FOCUSED, FAST & FLEXIBLE ENDORSEMENTS

"The VUCA world of volatility, uncertainty, complexity, and ambiguity is upon us—whether we like it or not. This book lays out the roadmap for surviving and prospering in these dynamic and challenging times."

Bob Seelert, Chairman Emeritus, Saatchi & Saatchi

"Even in the most successful organizations—danger lurks. It may take the form of complacency where maintaining the status quo, doing those things we have done well for years will continue to ensure our success even when we know the world around us and our competitive set continue to evolve at a much faster pace (VUCA). Tom and Nick helped prepare and mobilize our team for what lies around the corner— change and transformation at lightning speed. The Agile Model helped our managers see the world through the lens of opportunity—to anticipate what truly is around the next bend and to create resiliency for the challenges ahead...and winning in the marketplace."

Mark Nelson, President, ARAMARK Higher Education

"Nick Horney and Tom O'Shea have taken their extensive experience with CEOs and executive teams dealing with unprecedented change and complexity, and are sharing the lessons and tools with all of us. Focused, Fast and Flexible *is not a superficial 'how to,' but is instead a practical and comprehensive guidebook on sustainable change for today's leaders."*

Mary Eckenrod, VP Global Talent Management, Johnson Controls

"The fashion business, driven by consumer trend and innovation is already well immersed in VUCA and accelerating at an increasingly rapid pace. Successful companies of the future will need to be not only Focused, but Fast and Flexible at the same time. The Agile Model, outlined in Tom and Nick's book, provides the steps to competitive advantage in the future and coping with all aspects of VUCA."
Kevin Toomey, CEO, Kayser-Roth Corporation

"There is no question that the business environment is more turbulent than ever before. Tom O'Shea and Nick Horney have spent decades showing business leaders how to make sense out of these uncertainties. They can help you make certain that you and your company are not left behind."
Sandy Costa, author, *Humanity at Work: Encouraging Spirit, Achievement & Truth to Flourish in the Workplace*

"Nick and Tom switch our headlights to high-beams so we can see further down the road and prepare for multiple scenarios. This book provides an excellent model and practical guidelines for becoming an agile organization with agile leaders at every level. Read this book and incorporate its precepts into your leadership protocols, lest you become the proverbial 'deer in headlights' when unexpected shift happens. Put a copy in the hands of every leader at every level of your organization."
Joel Katz, President, Leadership Acumen

"While it is tempting and convenient to believe that change is so pervasive that people eventually adapt to it, the fact is that people are not naturally equipped or inclined to do that.

Understanding and leveraging the prescriptive approach explained in *The Agile Model* is an alternative path to acceptance, with a more likely outcome of resilience."

Jim Bowles, EdD, VP Leadership Practice, BTS USA

"If you were in the commercial banking industry during the recent financial crisis and Great Recession, you know that this cycle was a VUCA world on steroids. Our community bank began working with Tom O'Shea and the agility business model process at the onset of the crisis. I am convinced that Tom's work with our bank prepared and propelled us through the crisis in a manner that allowed us to not only survive, but thrive during the crisis. We were able to adapt to the changing conditions in a fast and cost-effective manner. We were able to remain flexible and re-align the organization as circumstances dictated. Best of all, we were able to engage the entire team in this process. The results were amazing!"

Kim D. Saunders, Retired President and CEO, M&F Bancorp and Mechanics & Farmers Bank

"The speed of play in business has been accelerating just like the speed of play in the major leagues of competitive sport. Business is definitely a team sport where speed, collaboration, creativity and adaptability are critical success factors and differentiators of winners and losers. Focused, fast and flexible are good descriptors for championship teams whether in the stadium or in corporate hallways. Tom and Nick's book captures the key insights to help any coach or leader build high performance, agile teams to win in today's competitive cauldron."

Anson Dorrance, Hall of Fame Head Women's Soccer Coach, UNC-Chapel Hill

"Working in high-growth entrepreneurial environments over the last two decades has absolutely confirmed the very real importance of proactive agility to me. Working focused and fast every day, in every situation, is now a hallmark of success in every organization, and especially where competition grows exponentially as in our direct sales industry. It is the CEO who is more than willing to change course—and quickly—that wins the race. But only if agility is organizationally developed as an internal track to run on."

Justo Nunez, VP Marketing, LIMU

"Today, every business is like a new arrival in a VUCA world, requiring different attitudes, skills, language and tools to survive. The Agile Model described in this book, and the mindset needed to execute it successfully, provides this needed guide. Backed up by logic, data and practical experience, Horney and O'Shea have eliminated the last excuses executives and their teams might have for failing to navigate their increasingly complex and fast moving world. The only question remaining is whether you are more agile than your competitors, because they are certainly not going to ignore agility as a fundamental business strategy."

Mark Haas, President, Research and Organization Management, former Chair of Institute of Management Consultants

FOCUSED, *FAST &* FLEXIBLE

CREATING
Agility Advantage
in a **VUCA World**

Nick Horney & Tom O'Shea

INDIE BOOKS
INTERNATIONAL

The Agile Model® is a registered trademark of Agility Consulting & Training, LLC.

ISBN: 1-941870-19-8
ISBN 13: 978-1-941870-19-8
Library of Congress Control Number: 2015935782

Designed by Joni McPherson, mcphersongraphics.com

INDIE BOOKS INTERNATIONAL, LLC
2424 VISTA WAY, SUITE 316
OCEANSIDE, CA 92054
www.indiebooksintl.com

Dedicated to Hampden D. Kenan—dear friend, mentor, futurist and philosopher who was responsible for our meeting in the first place. Bo, as his friends know him, has always been a provocateur of organizational possibilities. His thoughtful review and inputs to this manuscript were also provocative and valuable. Our thanks and appreciation.

CONTENTS

FOREWORD

The question of my career has been, "Why in business, despite all of our investments in strategic planning, business process re-engineering, leadership-development, team-building and goal-setting, amongst many other things, do we still experience a lot more wheel-spin than we should?" We struggle to gain traction on our desired trajectory of profit and growth. Rather than the breakthrough trajectory we desire, we find ourselves stuck with mild organic growth, or flat-lining, or worse, on the slippery slope of decline and a breakdown trajectory.

It is a question I have dedicated my career to understanding as a senior executive and then as CEO of the Aerospace Division of a British public company. Now, as a facilitator, mentor and coach of CEOs and their teams as well as a keynote speaker to Vistage International CEO groups worldwide, I help other executives unravel these issues to find that breakthrough trajectory.

The answer is always the same. Agility. Or rather, a lack of it. It doesn't matter whether I am working with start-ups to mature corporations; local, regional, national, international and global; private and public; high-tech and low-tech; new-economy and old-economy; for-profit and not-for-profit.

In my experience, the majority of leaders, teams and organizations are agility dis-advantaged. Why? Because they don't understand what agility is, let alone how to do it and who they need to be in the equation. They are left floundering in the disorganized-chaos of an increasingly dynamic and turbulent world. Far from being focused, fast and flexible, they are scattered, slow and stagnant. Fragile not agile.

There are those in the minority however, who are learning how to become agility-advantaged. Because they understand what agility is, how to institutionalize organizational-agility, build team-agility and who they need to be in the equation as role-models of leadership-agility. They too experience the chaos of an increasingly dynamic world, but as organized-chaos not disorganized-chaos. They have built out capabilities to recognize and face the rampant change defining today's environment with confidence, engagement, adaptability and nimbleness. They are focused, fast and flexible not scattered, slow and stagnant. Agile not fragile.

No two people understand the difference better than Nick Horney and Tom O'Shea. Our paths crossed in 2013 with such resonance that we joined forces. You have come to the right place to continue your journey from the majority to the minority. Enjoy this groundbreaking book.

Mike Richardson, author of *Wheel$pin: The Agile Executive's Manifesto*

THE JOURNEY BEGINS:

The Quest to be Focused, Fast and Flexible

While the pure essence of agility is found in three simple words (focused, fast, flexible), the path to a true agility advantage is a complex journey filled with opportunity and challenge. It starts with you as a leader and strategist whose job it is to make sense of a complicated and turbulent world and to respond to it better and faster than ever using new tools and constructs that create higher value , more engagement, and greater longevity for your enterprise.

We are living through the frenzy of innovation that is the hallmark of the twenty-first century, a century driven by the continuing digital revolution and rapidly expanding interconnectivity and intensifying global competition with radically evolving consumer expectations and dynamics. This environment of accelerated turbulence is not going to settle down—ever. Yale Professor Richard Foster has contended that we have entered the age where organizations and some leaders are becoming increasingly antiquated and even dysfunctional at record-setting speed. He projected that by the year 2020, more than three-quarters of the S&P 500 will be companies that we have not yet heard of in 2013. Of course, that means that an era of turbo turbulence is upon us, with increasingly vexing turmoil coming at us at increasing speed. Some have called this "accelerated obsolescence." We see this trend taking even more speed and casualties during the next decade.

There are several fundamental questions that leave survival hanging in the balance: How will organizations deal with such an environment? What will be the impact on your enterprise and how will you respond as a leader?

The clear answer is that you and your organization must become agile—focused, fast, and flexible—where the alignment of people, processes, and technology continuously adapt to changing conditions. This capability will enable you to continually anticipate, monitor, and adjust to trends and the new dynamics, so you and your enterprise not only survive but thrive.

There is a rapidly growing understanding by CEOs and senior leaders around the globe regarding the need for organizational agility, and many leaders have already attempted to promote it in their organizations in some form or fashion. All too often these attempts have fallen short because they only take aim at parts of the challenge, such as increasing speed to market with new products or enhancing employee engagement. But with a challenge this broad and complex, a systematic and holistic approach is necessary.

One of the axioms for understanding agility is that we must operate with an *AND paradigm*, and we must recognize that we cannot excel if we continue to think in terms of the trade-off propositions inherent in the *OR* paradigm. Understanding the difference between connection (and) versus alternatives (or) is critical in achieving organizational agility. We must be *fast* and *flexible*; we must have *flexibility* and *reliability*; we must have *quality* and *speed.* The list goes on in this uncompromising new age of agility. Our view of agility definitely fits this orientation and the understanding that one cannot create a la carte agility—just focusing on one aspect, driver, or domain—and meet today's demands. The lack of agility is an organizational illness whether leadership recognizes it or not. It cannot be isolated to just one area, function, or department. Agile organizations are healthy and vibrant throughout.

Organizations, like any natural organism, have always had to be sufficiently agile to adjust to changing environments or they risk their very existence. Agility is being increasingly discussed because today's environment is changing much faster than it used to, and faster than many organizations are capable of reacting. It is quite clear that the future will be defined by more of that same mind-numbing, often-conflicted organizational churn, with greater speed and more uncertainty. There is truth in the old observation that the only certainty is uncertainty— only more so today because there's more uncertainty than ever. The solution to the problem of making sure an organization can keep up is building the creative adaptability of the company. Organizations are faced with executing current strategies to survive today's challenges while remaining fluid enough to adapt to tomorrow's turbulence. Since executing and adapting requires many of the same resources, organizational leaders also face the dilemma of allocating people, processes, and technology to deliver goods and services, along with the equally vital need to invest for the long term to build a creatively adaptable, agile company. Most enterprises cannot find an elegant or even practical solution for this paradox. Those that do will be building potential for advantage.

In what follows, we will offer you an approach developed in the course of more than fifteen years of study working with dozens of organizations and thousands of leaders. We will describe a research-based, "next practice" model that frames the essential drivers of organizational agility, identifies the processes that enable each driver, and clarifies the domains and potential outcomes of a serious effort to become agile. We see The Agile Model as a next practice because we realize the model itself will continue to evolve; it has its own inborn agility. The framework of the model continues to stand the test of time for shaping what drives organizational agility while the how gets continuously replenished as we and others envision and create new tools and approaches for application.

We will also present a series of steps that you can follow—an essential roadmap—to begin to transform your organization into a more agile enterprise. The Agile Model and roadmap constitute a valuable resource for leaders at all levels—people like you who are seeking to pilot their organizations through daunting turbulence that only promises to increase. Companies around the globe are embracing agility and The Agile Model with accelerating pace. We are passionate about bringing its value, insights, and corresponding operating principles to you along with more than a decade's worth of practical experiences to help you build your own agility advantage.

SECTION ONE
The Agile Imperative

I n October 2008, Donna and David Van Eekeren looked at the widespread economic uncertainty around them and recognized that success and survival in the highly competitive packaged lunchmeat category with major mass retailers like Kroger and Walmart looked much the same—better, faster, and of course, more for less. Donna had already survived one major transition back in 2001 when she took over as CEO of Land O'Frost after the sudden passing of her husband, Paul. Now it was time for son David Van Eekeren to take the helm of this south-of-Chicago based, mid-size company and guide it to new heights. It was clear to both Donna and David that the company's long-standing commitment to quality and continuous improvement needed a new orientation—

agility. The competitive context and intensity had radically changed over the past decade making it clear that total company focus, nimbleness, and adaptability was an absolute for Land O'Frost's survival competing against the likes of Oscar Mayer and Sara Lee. This is the kind of clarity that led to the realization of the agile imperative and The Agile Model. Over the next three years, the Land O'Frost leadership team rallied to embrace agility and proceeded to apply the insights and learnings across the enterprise. They have continued to be the fastest growing lunchmeat brand in America.

CHAPTER 1

Navigating VUCA Turbulence

S ince that fateful day of September 11, 2001, made its indelible mark on history, the world has been experiencing a veritable roller coaster of extreme turbulence from a wide variety of forces of change: Mother Nature, sectarian blood conflicts, and sudden economic chaos, to name just a few. These are just a sampling of the negative forces of change percolating in the background.

Add the exponential explosion of possibilities from massive technological capabilities with their game-changing, disruptive implications, and include the innovation that's flooding the markets in industries like biotech, telecommunications, nanotechnology, pharma, agribusiness, and petrochemicals, and one might wonder if there's any hope for making sense of the discontinuity and disorder in the world.

Before getting to The Agile Model, it is useful to take a closer look at the turbulence it addresses. Dissecting the turmoil will help you better understand some of the dynamics in play—the operating context as well as the value proposition that emerges from exercising The Agile Model.

In the 1990s, social scientists working with the U.S. Army War College recognized the ongoing chaos happening around the world and the implications for their mission of preparing our military leaders to understand and lead in this context. They coined the acronym VUCA as a shorthand way of referring to this environment: **V**olatile, **U**ncertain, **C**omplex, and **A**mbiguous. After the tragedy of 9/11, many began to informally refer to the War College as VUCA University, signaling its realization that these were going to be long-term descriptors for the future realities that military leaders would face for some time to come. Since that time, VUCA has become increasingly well-known and adopted as the descriptor for the challenging internal and external environments that all organizations face today. Thus, VUCA is the context for the agility imperative and The Agile Model.

Today's daunting, ever-increasing speed of change is rapidly altering the relatively simple environment of the late twentieth century into a world of exponentially increasing turbulence. Being successful in this environ-ment requires a transformation in how an organization operates, in how it thinks about itself, and in how it is led. Each of the VUCA factors contributes significantly to the turbo turbulence in the operating context for leaders. Corporate leaders face the VUCA world every day. Today's leaders are now strapped into a world in which the need for comparable transformation in the leadership of organizations is an absolute necessity to match the level of change happening in competitive, consumer, customer, and workforce environments. Confident, agile organizations and leaders will be skillful guides able to convert the external negative energy into positive internal energy coursing down through the organization creating confidence and success by becoming more focused, fast and flexible. Let's take a closer look at the four key factors of VUCA.

➤ VOLATILITY

Volatility is experienced when an established order is changed or upset. Unexpected events occur. Expected events don't happen. New concepts surface that people aren't sure are true or don't know how to apply. Old ideas don't seem to work. The world has always experienced volatility to a certain extent, but the distance between today's realities and previous experience is widening at blinding speed. Until recently, society faced truly volatile times only periodically, based on significant social dislocations like major wars, serious epidemics, natural disasters, or broad economic crises. Today, widespread volatility is present on an almost constant basis, fueled by the growth of global connectivity, social media, interdependency, and often divisive parochial or ethnic agendas. The accelerating shift towards technology-driven globalization, hyper-communication, social networking, and intricate financial interdependencies sets up a future that is ripe for disruptive volatility and ongoing turbulence. What is the true capacity to predict the volatility ahead? Unfortunately, the tools to predict future volatility are not well developed in many organizations. Indeed, predicting instability has not been very good this past decade. The question is can it become better in the decades ahead?

Socio-political and economic volatility ripples through organizations in multitudes of ways, both directly and indirectly. The impact shows up in the form of potentially wild swings in availability of capital, markets, raw materials, and even travel and personal security. These dynamics influence the organization's risk profile and complexity of decision-making, as well as the implications for contingency planning as organizational leaders strive to anticipate potential scenarios. At a practical level, the volatility in the economy over the past decade has certainly resulted in a much more cautious business environment for large and small enterprise alike. Volatility naturally leads to uncertainty, which can impede confidence and speed for the average organization. But, volatility can also lead to opportunity for those who are focused, fast, and flexible competitors poised and positioned to seize resulting opportunities.

➤ UNCERTAINTY

Uncertainty is a state in which one isn't sure what is happening or will happen, and is unclear what if anything can be done. Uncertainty erodes one's sense of confidence and control. This feeling is particularly difficult for control-oriented managers. Uncertainty makes things much harder to predict and thus control. Where in the world (literally) will the next geopolitical, physical, or financial tsunami occur? And could the organization now get better prepared than it has been for some of the economic earthquakes of the past ten years? Contributing to the dynamic of uncertainty is the speed at which change can and is happening. The lead time of rampant change has been dramatically reduced, broadening the spectrum of possibilities that can come into play in an organization at any point in time. One of our clients likes to describe his solution for this uncertainty challenge as building skill throughout his organization for what he calls "the capability for looking around the corner."

Uncertainty can be paralyzing to organizations, contributing to the frozen-in-the-headlights syndrome that undermines some leaders and teams who sputter and stall into a malaise of inaction or delay that ultimately deteriorates competitive readiness. This uncertainty also takes a heavy toll on organizational confidence in the absence of active leadership communication and composure. We have seen many examples of waves of uncertainty crash across large organizations when new leaders take the helm or when some mergers or acquisitions suddenly obscure or change the previous ethos. There is a palpable lethargy that builds in organizations clouded by uncertainty. Lethargy and uncertainty are the anathema of agility.

➤ COMPLEXITY

Complexity occurs when there are many possible causes for any event and where cause and effect are unclear because challenges may seem too difficult to even define. Disorder plays out as an ever-growing intricacy of key interdependent decision factors, driven by the expanded number and interaction of component parts of critical processes. This complexity is fostered by growing specialization, larger institutions, hyper-technology, cultural nuances, and five hundred channels of digital and video content, along with multiple languages and generations. The list of possible causes is almost infinite and growing these days—some following linear thinking but many definitely not.

Complexity is a tsunami crashing against organizations creating corporate and individual casualties by drowning those who get overwhelmed or are incapable of finding ways to get on top of the wave. This factor of growing complexity may be the most perplexing dynamic hindering corporate speed and fluidity in the current era and beyond. Since 2012 IBM Global Services has regularly interviewed over 1,500 global CEOs to better understand the issues they faced and expected to face in the future. This notion of complexity is often raised as one of the most significant challenge—one they expected to become more and more significant in the future.

Complexity is also a challenge that these CEOs declared required great advances in what they called leadership creativity and organizational dexterity. The fact is that many leadership solutions learned in the past are often not applicable to the challenges faced in the current era— most now require fresh creative thinking and a capacity to mobilize organizations to adapt, change, and accelerate.

The complexity dynamic has clearly become exponential as it multiplies the effects of the other VUCA factors, creating a more chaotic concoction of realities for leaders to navigate. Those organizations and leaders who are able to create high coefficients of clarity around their value propositions, organizational values, and strategic priorities will be better able to make complexity management through organizational dexterity a competitive advantage.

We will spend time later in this book, beginning in chapter 5 with visioning and then in chapter 7 by creating a bias for action and looking at specific and practical ways you and your leaders can develop the fitness of focus, speed, and flexibility that produces the dexterity to survive and prosper in this world of exponential change.

➤ AMBIGUITY

Ambiguity occurs when there are multiple possible meanings or alternatives for a given situation or event, so things such as right or wrong, good or bad aren't as self-evident or clear. Organizational life may sometimes be compared to one of those high-speed photos that make everything look like a blur. One can't quite make out the right answer or even get everyone to agree on what they see in the photo. When there is a lack of clarity about what is right or wrong, good or bad, true or false, trustworthy or not, it is then that ambiguity exists and agility sputters.

Ambiguity is especially debilitating when it distorts the clarity of corporate values and priorities. How many corporate debates are centered around what should be done next only to discover the range of possibilities crosses many lines depending upon how badly corporate needs the sales that month.

Organizations often create their own ambiguity through the mixed signals they send that disconnect corporate stated vision, values, and strategies with actual managerial behaviors. They say their people are their most valuable asset, but then implement policies or practices that do not live out those statements. They say customer satisfaction is their highest strategic priority, but then approve shipping orders earlier than customers request or want so they can show sales before year end in order to make max bonus.

All of the aspects of turbo turbulence, from shifting consumer preferences to the seesaw of political party influence and the myriad of other examples, come into play when considering ambiguity. The combined force and impact from continuous volatility, uncertainty, and the growing complexity all around us contribute to this ambiguity. In fact, each of these factors has a part to play in the other three.

Ambiguity can also involve vagueness about your own current situation, in addition to the vagueness or ambiguity about your desired or expected outcomes. Finding ways to eliminate as much ambiguity as possible about your vision for your organization—together with making an objective assessment of your current state—is an important first step for you in coping and building a strategic journey to adapt and thrive against the VUCA impact.

One question to consider is: How do we evaluate the risks and consequences from taking one course of action versus another? Reflect on whether the ground rules and paradigms used in the past to help guide decision-making are giving the right answers in these circumstances.

➤ THE AGILITY ADVANTAGE: KEY TO SURVIVING IN A VUCA WORLD?

Each organization faces its own indigenous VUCA climate and context—we call it your VUCAsphere. We believe VUCA is here for the long term, so the critical response is for organizations to develop a superior capacity to recognize and evaluate the VUCA factors as the organizations continue to serve their stakeholders.

Building this capacity becomes the operating context for creating agility for your organization, and before we go any further, we should define what we mean by organizational agility. We see organizational agility as a superior capacity to deliver stakeholder success in an increasingly VUCA world by sensing and responding to obstacles and opportunities better and faster than competition at all levels of your organization. Organizations able to deliver on that proposition will have a clear advantage—a truly competitive advantage for however long it takes your competition to catch up. A true agility advantage will be very hard for others to replicate and hence overcome.

These VUCA contextual factors will ultimately set the bar for what being agile actually means. It is not unlike categorizing conditions in whitewater rafting or rating the force of hurricanes. Are you and your team navigating through Class 1 or Class 5 rapids? Are you operating in storm conditions that are Category 1 or Category 5? In addition to understanding the nature of your challenge, you'll want to know about the readiness of your vessel (business model, value proposition, processes, and technology) and your crew (your leadership, culture, and people). How would you rate your agility? Are you Class One—Agility Novice or Class Five—Agility Master? We will discuss this evolution and agility development in greater detail once we have covered more of the background. The Agile Model, explained in detail in the following chapters, along with the associated lessons and practical tools, are intended as a companion's guide for your journey, a journey that will help make you and your organization more focused, fast, and flexible.

CHAPTER 2

Embracing The Agile Model

W hat does it take for you and your organization to develop the capabilities to regularly sense and respond better and faster at all levels and become agile? We created a model based on a combination of insights from more than a decade of progressive research, combined with widespread practical experience, that led us to conclude organizational agility is powered by five critical drivers embodied in the **Anticipate/Generate/Initiate/Liberate/Evaluate (AGILE) Model** and applied actively across three enterprise domains (people, processes, and technology) to create a dynamic outcome. That outcome is the creation of focused, fast, and flexible organizations poised for success in a VUCA world.

During the course of writing this book, we engaged a kind and thoughtful man named Martin Wilcox, former head of publications at the Center for Creative Leadership in Greensboro, North Carolina. Martin has a penchant for asking simple but very important questions like, "Since you have been helping clients for over a dozen years with this agility stuff, what differentiates those who get it from those who don't?" After only about a minute of reflection, the answer was quite clear—a certain core belief system.

The Agile Model was originally developed by Nick Horney in 2001 after leaving the Center for Creative Leadership and founding Agility Consulting & Training (ACT). It was further refined with Tom O'Shea in 2003 into its present form after Nick and Tom merged their consulting practices. The Agile Model delineates the five key drivers of agility supported by the identification of fifteen core agility capabilities and

FIGURE 1.1

seventy-five corresponding organizational competencies to be developed in agile organizations and leaders. The Agile Model has been recognized as the "best leadership model for our changing times" and is increasingly cited in articles and publications for its applicability and value. In June 2012, Dr. Karl Moore, from McGill University in Canada, writing in *Forbes* declared that "agility is the defining ingredient in next generation leadership" and recognized The Agile Model as a framework for success that future leaders can use as a developmental roadmap.

➤ THE AGILE MODEL DRIVERS

In The Agile Model, agility for organizations, teams and leaders is driven by five critical abilities: **A**nticipating change, **G**enerating confidence, **I**nitiating action, **L**iberating thinking, and **E**valuating results.

The ability to **anticipate change** requires you to pay systematic attention to multiple contextual elements (both internal and external): the general environment, including economic, political, and cultural developments; specifics of your business, including technical issues and the dynamics of customer demands; and organizational factors, including strategy, finances, structure, and business practices. You must have effective processes for visioning, sensing, and monitoring.

The ability to **generate confidence** requires you to address issues related to how your people, internal and external to your organization, understand and feel about their capacities, and the dynamics involved with creating satisfaction for all of your organization's stakeholders. Personal awareness of strengths and developmental needs is the starting point for self-confidence and one's capability to generate confidence. Much of this rests squarely on your ability to inspire trust, commitment, communication, and involvement in all stakeholders—internally and externally—building the DNA of your culture and values through actions. You must have effective processes of connecting, aligning, and engaging.

The ability to **initiate action** requires you to assure that within your organization there is an inclination toward proactive action as well as the means to advance focused activity reasonably and promptly. You must have a shared mindset and effective processes for creating that bias for action and sense of urgency, for improving active and widespread decision-making, and for actively collaborating with internal and external stakeholders.

The ability to **liberate thinking** requires you to assure that your organization has the means to originate and incorporate new ideas. You must have effective processes that build capacity and energy for innovation, also creating that inclination towards, and bias for, innovation, focusing on customers to provide the fuel for innovation, and generating meaningful concept diversity from high levels of idea engagement with all stakeholders. This driver is essentially concerned with creating a supportive environment to build capacity and energy for innovation.

The ability to **evaluate results** requires you to align vision to action, acquiring the knowledge and facts necessary to learn from and improve the actions you and your organization take. You must have effective processes for creating expectations aligned to your success model, providing real-time feedback throughout the value chain and with your people, and identifying and utilizing fact-based measures that link each part of the organization to an overall success map. The after-action-review process is a best practice illustration from the military that is often missing in private-sector organizations.

Each driver is a vital force, yet applying only some of them or each one individually won't make your organization truly agile. For example, having a focused effort to anticipate change does little to enhance overall organizational agility if there is not a sense of urgency to initiate action based on the trends and patterns of changes identified. Action can be initiated through the deliberate enhancement of marketplace monitoring tools. A corporate initiative to generate confidence in all employees through an employee-engagement survey cannot achieve the potential offered by organizational agility without providing employees with an understanding of the business strategy and ensuring a culture that's supportive of liberated thinking.

➤ AGILITY CORE BELIEF SYSTEM

In many respects, the commitment to a model of organizational agility involves the adoption of a new operating system, much like upgrading and transforming your computer from an inadequate operating system like the old Vista operating system into the latest and greatest. Just as the demands in speed, memory capacity, and multifunctioning platforms of today's technology requirements far outstripped the capabilities of those earlier versions, the demands of the technology-driven VUCA world have been making certain leaders and many organizations obsolete. Introducing and building a commitment to an Agile Operating System—an AOS—first requires a commitment to a set of fundamental principles. Outlined in this chapter are some of the shared values and beliefs that must be understood and adopted as starting points when exploring a commitment to building an agile organization.

Arduous as your journey to agility may be, taking three to five years at least, it will help you create a stronger culture and organization fully prepared for the VUCA world. From the beginning, the length of your journey to get on the path will be determined by how close your existing value system and culture align with the tenets outlined here. Said another way, your gain will be well worth any pain inherent in the process.

Those leaders or clients who believe strongly in a clear set of tenets tend to understand better and get more agility traction than those who do not buy in to this belief system. Here are the core beliefs an organization needs to become agile.

AGILITY CORE BELIEF SYSTEM

The world will continue to move faster and get more volatile, uncertain, complex, and ambiguous (VUCA) in the future—a lot more.

Agility is not just nice to do. It is imperative for survival and a competitive advantage opportunity in a VUCA world.

Your people are the highest priority. They are the basis of your adaptability and the key to customer satisfaction. Providing them the opportunity to grow and develop is paramount.

The members of your organization must all share a mindset of commitment to being focused, fast, and flexible, fueled by achieving excellence in the five drivers of The Agile Model.

The agile culture elements are vital to success: caring, connecting, committed, challenging, curious, and creating.

The operating principles that help shape organizational agility include simplicity, speed, synchronicity, fluidity, modularity, and scalability.

The tenets of the Agility Core Belief System represent a mental model that senior leadership and ultimately your entire organization must share to make this journey successful. These tenets are important ingredients in the overall equation for creating and sustaining agility. Variability within the leadership cadre in the extent of these beliefs will directly influence the pace of change and development of adaptive capabilities.

We discussed the framework of the VUCA world in chapter 1. The years ahead will be filled with accelerating and rampant change, but will all of your key leaders recognize this reality and share in the conclusion that making corporate agility strategic is an absolute? If they do not, this variability in leadership team alignment has to be reconciled or the progress of building speed and adaptability will be undermined, creating greater drag and confusion within the organization. These dynamics will be covered in more detail in section 2. But make no mistake, each one of the elements in the Agility Core Belief System is critical to your long-term success.

CHAPTER 3

Leveraging the Big Three: People, Process, and Technology

For agility to be most efficiently achieved within your organization, The Agile Model and the Agility Core Belief System must be applied in the three major domains for any organization: people, processes, and technology.

During the past dozen years, we have seen reams of studies and data published about the definitive role of people in driving superior results in organizations. As evidenced by the Agility Core Belief System, we believe people are paramount in the agility creation equation. The works of James Heskett, Gary Loveman and others in *The Service Profit Chain*, as well as John Fleming's and Jim Asplund's *Human Sigma*, and, more recently, Scott Keller's and Colin Price's work *Beyond Performance*, clearly highlight not just the power of people, but also the fact that significantly engaging people within organizations can lead to more than three times the productivity of average employee teams. Similar research indicates that as much as 40 percent of employee productivity is actually discretionary, meaning there is a very large part of the average employee's productivity within an organization that he or she can choose to give or not. The choice is mostly dependent on the leadership culture and organizational value system. We believe the ideal organization culture for supporting agility development is characterized by caring, connecting, committing, challenging, curiosity, and creating.

➤ PEOPLE AS PRIORITY

Organizations that are truly agile will continuously focus on their people as a distinguishing priority and as a strategically powerful differentiator. So, how do these culture factors play into creating the agility dynamic? Here's an outline of some of the rationale and benefits of the agile culture:

SHAPING THE CULTURE FOR AGILITY

CARING	• Agile organizations build a culture of mutual caring in the enterprise core value system. Success for the company and the team, as well as other stakeholders, matter. • Creating a culture that cares involves building high trust, respect, and openness.
CONNECTING	• Active collaboration is one of the most important features of agile organizations and leaders. It is the engine for action, fostering widespread inclusiveness. • Agile organizations build the muscle of capability through collaboration that leverages each of the other elements in the agile culture.
COMMITTING	• Agile organizations succeed through fulfilling commitments better and faster at all levels, building ownership and accountability. • Focus and speed for the enterprise are highly dependent upon reliability in commitments.
CHALLENGING	• Candor and a climate of openness to encourage positive challenging of status quo is very hard, but essential, for creating agile organizations with better and faster solutions flowing at all levels. • Agile organizations can never be complacent in that we know we must find better and faster solutions continuously or else we fail or worse—we create organizational malaise incapable of winning.
CURIOSITY	• Curiosity drives us to build our situational intelligence involving customers, competitors, community, supply partners, and all stakeholders.
CREATING	• Agile organizations and its people are proactive, not passive, demonstrating initiative and resourcefulness to create added value for company and customers.

Another reality or paradox is this: just as an organization's people can be its greatest asset and competitive advantage, sometimes people can be the biggest obstacles to its agility because the need to change often involves significant transformation for some within the workforce and can represent the most complex aspect of the agility journey. Increasingly, it is widely recognized that the battle for the right kind of talent has high stakes and will be a clear critical success factor for as far as we can see.

➤ BUSINESS PROCESSES AND OPERATING PRINCIPLES

The meticulous analysis and restructuring of business operating principles, structures, and processes are often the least understood and valued parts of the effort to promote agility. The work is not glamourous, yet, it is the everyday business processes that define most of what gets done. The rapidly changing business environment requires new biases and filters that offer a fresh look at business-process engineering. How many leaders outside of the manufacturing zone have applied the disciplines in Lean Six Sigma to track the value creation in core business processes or authorized search-and-destroy missions to find obsolete or non-value-added processes? Every day, routine processes are often the source of much drag in organizations, hindering speed and fluidity with conflicting, ambiguous, or dysfunctional processes that have been patched and poorly bandaged over years of organizational downsizing and restructuring.

Organizations committed to becoming more agile must take a fresh look at each of the elements in the classic organization design mix such as Jay Galbraith's STAR model: strategy, structure, processes, rewards, and people. How do these five elements contribute or inhibit your organization's agility? How do they support your drive to be more focused, fast, and flexible across your enterprise? These considerations become increasingly important as you examine how to help your globally distributed organization be successful in a world where speed, collaboration, and complexity dominate. Organizational structure and processes should be guided by operating principles that emphasize speed, simplicity, reliability, synchronicity, fluidity, modularity, and connectivity. As organizations develop in valuing the outcomes of being focused, fast, and flexible, they must examine these operating principles through process design or reengineering.

OPERATING PRINCIPLES FOR SHAPING AGILITY

SPEED	• Speed matters more and more every day, largely driven by the give-it-to-me-now-for-less consumer mentality that dominates every aspect of business and life. Speed is important in business but not at the cost of quality. Better and faster—not merely faster—is the agile mantra.
SIMPLICITY	• There is so much complexity crushing business operators today that it makes the goal of simplifying business models and processes have extra high value. Simple is more elegant and reliable.
SYNCHONICITY	• Timing and alignment are becoming increasingly important aspects of agility, especially as they relate to interacting with ever-changing customers and consumers' expectations.
FLUIDITY	• Continuous flow brings the highest efficiency and energy into your business model. Flow and throughput are concepts that can operate across every aspect of your business model. Finding what inhibits or obstructs your flow and throughput of consumer demand, order processing, manufacturing process, or even idea generation will improve your fluidity
MODULARITY	• Plug-and play-modularity enhances adaptability, scalability, and convenience. USB devices provides a good example of agile modularity. How many devices have become accessible and simplified through USB magic? How can you apply USB concepts in your business?
CONNECTIVITY	• One of the elements in the Apple success story is attributed to its interconnectedness. All devices and components can talk to each other and give and receive feedback, energy, information, and mystique. How can you apply these concepts in your business?

In our discussion of implementation in section 2, we offer approaches for examining the efficacy of organizational processes for building an agile enterprise using a variety of agility diagnostic assessment tools.

➤ TECHNOLOGY RULES

No domain has experienced, or will experience, more rapid, rampant, and continuous change than the field of technology—better, faster, cheaper, more mobile, multi-platformed, synchronous—the beat goes on. Technology can absolutely accelerate performance enhancement. There have been numerous examples of competitive leapfrogging via new technology capabilities: Google, Skype, and Amazon are some of the best-known, high-value cases. But on smaller scales, that leapfrogging is happening every day. Customer expectations around speed, convenience, transparency, and flexibility require most organizations to continuously challenge how they leverage technology. The on-going explosion of interest and use of agile methodology in software and IT development offers another excellent illustration of how the fusion of people, process, and technology considerations come together to provide enhanced speed and greater stakeholder connectivity. Technology operates at every level—customer, supplier, employee, competitors, regulatory, and shareholders—in most organizational realms.

Every single day we are seeing almost revolutionary advances that just five or ten years ago would have been unthinkable. Technology has become an enabler and in many cases a game changer. The advent of over five hundred thousand apps on Apple and Android handheld devices and the flood of continuous invention enable new business opportunities as well as massive productivity improvement. How many small businesses have been started via internet that would otherwise not exist? How has the invention of a credit card swipe attachment for smart phones suddenly solved a core commercial process for small business? The list is endless and the future possibilities beyond our imagination. But not everyone's.

Organizations are adopting and adapting technology changes in a variety of ways and speed. Technology is enabling leapfrog acceleration of competitive advantage where the smaller tech-savvy competitor is able to jump over other competitors that lack the speed, customization, or added value that technology can sometimes bring. The table outlining operating principles for shaping agility applies to technology as well. Technology is necessary to help organizations create speed, simplicity, synchronicity, fluidity, modularity, and interconnectivity.

To achieve organizational agility, you must align the work you do with your people, your processes, and your technology with each of the five drivers–anticipating change, generating confidence, initiating action, liberating thinking and evaluating results. If there are major inconsistencies, your organization may achieve only limited success. On the other hand, your challenge is to innovate with your people, process and technology to invigorate the five drivers, your organization will be able to continuously learn and create new and greater value for all stakeholders, regardless of changes in the marketplace.

CHAPTER 4

Seizing the Agility Advantage

C reating an advantage assumes competitors exist in the marketplace. It also demands organizational capabilities to sense and respond better and faster to ever changing customer expectations as well as competitor capabilities by being more focused, fast, and flexible at all levels in your organization and in your relationships with all your stakeholders. Agility is at the heart of your strategy for creating competitive advantage. Agility capabilities must operate at all levels within and connected to your organization—learn how to seize the agility advantage in this chapter.

➤ BEING FOCUSED

Begin by learning to focus. The word *focus* goes back to the Latin word *foci*, which means the convergence of light rays to create fire. That definition offers more than just the clarity aspect typically implied in focus, it also shows a resulting outcome from taking focused action. Fire represents the kind of enabler for action and outcomes that characterizes focused and agile organizations. In a similar way, we often hear the phrase "burning platform" to describe a strong sense of purpose and call to action. Although there has been an explosion of technology tools to help improve personal and corporate productivity in the real-time world, there is no substitute for focus and the basic understanding of the value proposition that differentiates your business from the competition. Apple's revolutionary iPod phenomenon, which was developed as a result of having both a continual focus on consumer lifestyles and a dedication to finding the important lifestyle-related trends in consumer daily life patterns, influences, and needs of its core and very loyal consumer franchise. This is an excellent example of applying focus and understanding to the value proposition of a business.

Focus might also be *the* most overused and least understood word in today's business vocabulary, yet it remains the largest lever for increasing speed and responsiveness. In 2007, the American Management Association published a study on *The Keys to Strategy Execution* that clearly demonstrated the high correlation between financially successful organizations and those with high ratings for clarity of mission and message. When leaders keep consistent focus on the vital few priorities and align the appropriate resources to match those priorities, the essential conditions for success are in place.

What is the focus of your organization? Focus relates to a discussion about strategic objectives but also has just as much to do with organizational values. Agile organizations create an elegant partnership when what the organization does and how it does it operate as an inseparable combination. When ambiguity about priorities and/or values exists within the organization, speed and commitment regarding performance often become casualties. Increasingly, organizations around the globe are beginning to dial up clarity on key operating principles to guide management actions instead of detailed rules to control and conform because today's organizations are too global and too complex to prescribe every rule for every transaction in every situation. Focused organizations strive to build and project clarity at the highest levels around vision, values, operating principles, strategic capabilities and priorities. Organizations become what they tolerate. Focus must have an accountability obligation if it is to be sustainable. Focus sets the stage for organizations to then become fast and flexible.

If your efforts to focus your organization on the vital few priorities are going to bear fruit, you must be clear on both *what* is to be done and *how* things are to be done with regard to values and operating principles. The whole organization has to be clear on vision, values, and operating principles to shape the future of that vision.

CHARACTERISTICS OF FOCUSED AND UNFOCUSED ORGANIZATION

Focused Organizations	Unfocused Organizations
• Consistently attain high customer satisfaction scores	• Chronically receive low customer survey scores
• Consistently achieve high participation rates on customer surveys	• Probably do not have regular customer surveys or customer satisfaction measures
• Consistently attain key objectives; maintain a culture of accountability and commitment	• Consistently fall short on key objectives; low trust level in commitments made
• Create highly visible, real-time key performance indicators for every function and location	• Lack consistent or visible metrics; could be measuring things rather than priorities
• Establish an active and aligned performance feedback system for all team members	• Use performance reviews inconsistently or simply avoid them; viewed by the troops as a punishment system
• Actively measure internal customer satisfaction across all areas of organization	• Lack an awareness or culture for satisfying internal customers; have high conflict silos

➤ BEING FAST

Tom O'Shea played and coached soccer for many, many years. As a youth soccer coach, Tom developed a realization that there are two major aspects to speed of young soccer players. How fast are they and when did they start running. The key to helping players, young or old, improve speed is helping them read the game better so they might take one or two steps before their opponents react. This helps make them net, net faster and we live in a net, net world. The same proposition applies to leaders, teams, and organizations looking to increase speed and agility to sense and respond better and faster.

Fast is important. As Dr. Gary Hamel wrote in his classic *Harvard Business Review* article, "The Quest for Resilience," "The only dependable advantage is a superior capacity to reinvent your business model before circumstances force you to." Accelerated obsolescence is certainly putting this notion to a real test. Both your customers and their customers continuously expect and demand the next innovation that will increase value or convenience, and have come to expect innovation in real-time or even quicker. The idea that speed matters is becoming increasingly prevalent even in industries that once seemed somewhat immune to this dynamic. Organizations and leaders able to adapt and adjust, similar to the way a NASCAR driver weaving through the crowded track at 200 mph acclimates to change, will be well-positioned to succeed.

For speed to be beneficial, an organization must become faster than the competition at what really matters. It is not a matter of always being faster at everything. Speed is also a relative measure—after all, how fast is fast? Often your customers and competitors will determine that for you. Historically, organizations are more likely to measure speed primarily in the manufacturing environments. However, in the current hypercompetitive world, speed matters every step of the way. From recognizing emerging trends and decision-making loops to all aspects of your innovation processes, fast is not only expected, it is demanded.

CHARACTERISTICS OF FAST AND SLOW ORGANIZATIONS

Fast Organizations	Slow Organizations
• Have built a culture with an expectation for action and widespread sense of urgency	• Have built a culture where urgency is not valued or where lack of clarity on priorities befuddles the need for speed
• Have established and connected good mechanisms for sensing and monitoring the forces of change in order to recognize trends and act faster	• Have not established "early alert system" to help them become more proactive, so they spend most of the time fire-fighting and reacting to whatever comes first
• Get new products or services to their customers better and faster than others	• Find themselves missing growth opportunities and having to more often trim margins to compete
• Have identified where speed matters and created metrics to track and educate	• Tend to focus only on internal efficiencies and miss customer and market perspectives
• Recognize that quality and reliability drives speed so they strive to be better and faster	• Have not built a quality-first culture and lack the discipline that enables speed and adaptability

➤ BEING FLEXIBLE

"Society is undergoing enormous structural change and the accelerated rate of technological and social change will overwhelm people, leaving them feeling disconnected and suffering shattering stress and disorientation": This could have easily been written anytime in the past decade but, in fact, this is part of the introduction to Alvin Toffler's visionary book *Future Shock*, written in 1970. Overwhelming change has just about become the new normal in the 21st century, which makes the need for adaptability and flexibility paramount for both individuals and organizations. The corporate graveyard is full of individuals and companies that could not or would not adapt as change demands— sometimes through stubbornness and sometimes through lack of either vision or awareness that change was necessary.

Organizational flexibility sustains true competitiveness. There are many examples of companies, and even industries that were not able to anticipate and respond effectively to change fast enough to survive. One such example hits close to our home in Greensboro, North Carolina, which is one of the major centers for the apparel and textile industry and once headquarters for Burlington Industries. In the late 1990s, Burlington Industries was a multi-billion dollar textile industry leader with over eighty thousand employees. The company lost its edge, shrank in size and progressively declined such that it no longer exists as a standalone entity, disappearing into the Wilbur Ross-led industry roll-up in 2003. On March 2,

2008, Greensboro witnessed the dramatic implosion of the iconic Burlington Industries headquarters building. The property has been transformed into an upscale shopping center, which includes an Apple store that is flourishing at that location. This is a poignant example of one company failing to adequately adapt versus another that is a leader in adaptability.

Too many organizations today harbor the notion of a flexibility paradox that an organization cannot have organizational flexibility and disciplined processes at the same time. There are people who believe that disciplined processes actually hamstring flexibility and prevent organizations from adapting to change. This is simply not true. The Agile Model helps organizations achieve flexibility by demystifying forces of change, building confidence and commitment to purpose, increasing capability to shift directions using fresh, innovative thinking and more.

The key to flexibility is found in a combination of people, processes, and technology. Flexibility begins with a mindset formed with the CORE BELIEF SYSTEM, understanding that adaptability is a survival strategy. Agile organizations understand that this notion of psycho-sclerosis—a hardening of the attitudes about change—greatly inhibits organizational flexibility.

Embedding the Agility Core Belief System we introduced earlier for agile culture and agile operating principles will help you build the kind of flexibility needed to face the VUCA future.

CHARACTERISTICS OF FLEXIBLE AND INFLEXIBLE ORGANIZATIONS

Flexible Organizations	Inflexible Organizations
• Recognize that change and the need for adaptability are realities to be expected	• Often operate in a state of denial believing the good old days will return soon
• Examine their business models to identify and challenge areas limiting flexibility	• Confuse building flexibility with adding complexity, variability, and cost
• Adopt and employ agility-building design concepts like simplicity, modularity, fluidity, and synchronicity	• Do not see flexibility as a serious consideration influencing strategy, business portfolio, or organization design
• Invest in building flexibility via people, process and technology including cross-training, collaborationfocus, and greater mobility in IT	• Stay more centrally controlling in decision-making, information management, and resource allocation
• Recognize and support importance of a health scorecard approach to defining and measuring success with key agility indicators	• Tend to more narrowly define success often in basic financial terms only, lacking recognition of customers, employees, or the need to invest in capacity to innovate

The alignment and interaction of all of these constructs are what builds the agility advantage. People, processes, and technology all working together to support achievement of success measures better and faster are the keys to an agile enterprise.

KEYS TO BUILDING AN AGILE ENTERPRISE

AGILITY GOALS	PEOPLE	PROCESS	TECHNOLOGY
FOCUSED	• How do you insure your people understand and are engaged on key organization priorities • Leadership team has a high degree of shared clarity and accountability for improvement	• Do you have clarity for the owners of mission critical processes and how well they meet customer requirements?	• How well does your technology support critical processes and enterprise value proposition? • How does it compare with competition?
FAST	• Does your organizational climate reinforce sense of urgency for doing right things? • Do you facilitate speed of decision making by empowering team members with skills and authority?	• Do your mission critical business processes provide you competitive advantage or disadvantage?	• Where does your technology provide you competitive speed advantage? • Where are you at clear speed disadvantage because of technology?
FLEXIBLE	• What is the capacity of your workforce to adapt to change. • Is your organization agile or fragile as it relates to major factors that can disrupt your success?	• Do you measure critical process speed and flow? • What is the scalability of your critical processes? • How modular are your processes to transfer or operate in field?	• What is the extent of user involvement in technology applications? • Are you able to adapt technology solutions to portfolio differences? • Have you embraced mobility as a technology strategy?

➤ A ROADMAP FOR IMPLEMENTING AGILITY

There are many dimensions of agility within organizations —individual agility, leadership agility (like supply chain or sales), team agility, strategic agility, and functional agility, to name only a few. The Agile Model will help you concentrate on all of these dimensions, integrate your efforts to address them, and draw on the work of many experts. But in order to incorporate the dimensions effectively and to transform your organization into a truly agile enterprise, you and everyone in your organization must commit to following a roadmap that will guide your journey.

The journey will not be easy, but it is easy enough to understand. It takes five steps: (1) mobilize, in which you prepare the organization for the journey; (2) envision, in which you establish a clear idea of the organization's current situation (where it is) and project its desired state (where it wants to go in the near term); (3) plan, in which you determine specifically how to get the organization from where it is to where it wants to be; (4) deploy, in which you implement the measures that will move the organization to the desired state; and (5) sustain, in which you keep renewing the purposes of the first four steps and refreshing the journey for new VUCA in the marketplace.

For each step there are specific actions that are important and our model will help you navigate. When you follow this roadmap, and if you pay particular attention to your organization's agility culture and supportive operating principles, you will be able to guide your enterprise successfully through the VUCA world.

As we introduce each of the agile drivers in the following chapters, we also provide practical tips for exploring and learning and applying the various aspects involved in the journey to greater agility. The Agile Model is a highly effective framework for facing the future and building competitive advantage in organizational capability. It is also a framework that can embrace and accommodate other work in the fields of organization and leadership development, especially with the ever-evolving push for innovation as organizations anticipate change, generate confidence, initiate action, liberate thinking, and evaluate results better and faster than ever.

The next section offers a more detailed description of The Agile Model and the roadmap. It concludes with some observations about the changing world, discusses how to begin the process for becoming a more agile enterprise, and emphasizes the urgent need for organizations to change in response to the fast pace while staying focused and flexible.

SECTION TWO:
A Guided Tour of The Agile Model

I n August 2003, it was hot and steamy in Cary, North Carolina, but Mark Nelson, then Southeast Region Vice President for ARAMARK Higher Education, knew the real heat was still ahead as he recognized the significant change looming for his organization over the next couple of years. Mark, now president of this $2.5 billion provider of managed services for dining, convenience stores, facilities management, and conference centers at major United States colleges and universities, could see his major clients already becoming much more demanding and at the same time a number of his senior leaders were getting ready for retirement. He often described his biggest challenge as helping his team improve skills at looking around the corner and being ready for what they would find there. Over the next decade, he and his team became much more attuned to the drivers of agility and building the capability to look around that corner. They also found ways to continuously lead the overall corporation in key performance metrics in an industry that experienced dramatic change from new learning formats (like University of Phoenix) along with the on-going squeeze of state budget funding cuts of higher education. Agility matters, just ask Mark.

CHAPTER 5

A is for Anticipating Change

C hange is the new normal operating context and it is synchronous and disruptive with all of the VUCA factors percolating a challenging new brew every day. Unexpected events occur, expected ones don't, and conditions vary significantly. Change is something that no one, and no organization, can ignore. If all is going well, people fear change. If things are not going well, people hope for change. Either way, you and your enterprise need to deal with it.

The best way to deal with change is through clear-eyed anticipation. Anticipating change has become a rigorous endeavor for those serious about staying competitive in a rapidly changing global environment. Professor Don Sull from the London School of Business describes the current corporate visibility or capability to see into the future in his book, *The Upside of Turbulence* as the fog of the future where all knowledge is provisional. What he means is the world has become sufficiently volatile and uncertain, making the past paradigms we used to guide our actions only provisionally valid in helping us navigate today's increasingly foggy future. Sull is very clear in saying, "Not only do we not know what the future holds. . . we *can't* know what the future holds," and trying to predict too far out can cause some seriously bad decisions. The key to driving consistently reliable execution is to create a shared belief system or culture within your organization that excels in sensing and responding better and faster to the rapidly changing conditions.

Technology, globalization, demographics, security, and consumer demand for more choices and convenience all contribute to making today's society one of accelerating change. The drivers of change are numerous and complex, and their impact varies from one sector to another. Adapting too late or too little can result in radical measures such as large-scale downsizing, hostile take-overs, rushed mergers, or as described earlier, can result in obsolescence. In today's unstable economic climate, companies that succeed in integrating agility into their business strategy in an informed way will have a competitive advantage. Anticipating change is not just building foresight to identify possible future scenarios as a first step in preparing for change and managing it successfully. These steps are important, but agility is much more fluid and dynamic in striving to create capabilities that can sense changes in your competitive environment and respond swiftly in ways that are better and faster at *all levels* in your organization.

You might think about anticipating change as building smart organizations in much the same fashion as smart technology tools are able to rapidly sense patterns and trends in user behavior to dynamically prompt your next progressive action such as your smart phone completing your sentences. The fluidity in your capability to anticipate change before evident to others will contribute greatly to your success and minimize obstacles and resistance that could limit the possibilities of your people, processes, and technology.

Anticipating change isn't predicting the future or predicting the unpredictable. In fact, it derives from the ability to project what is expected and to thereby see the forces of change and how those forces might play out. Anticipating change depends on having a schematic understanding of your organization, the conditions and forces that affect it, the insight for how these will interact in dynamic ways while envisioning various outcomes. As forces and conditions change, so will outcomes. The paradigm shift for agile organizations is the realization that they cannot predict a singular, specific view of the future. The real point of competitive differentiation comes to those enterprises that can engage and include the full organization into a dynamic, super-sensory body with widespread capability for understanding forces of change at all levels—in both personal and corporate ways.

Because the dynamics of each organization's VUCAsphere will ultimately determine success, the processes for anticipating change need to define your unique organizational focus and the context so you can, systematically gauge how they are playing out, and detect how important factors may affect predictability. The essential processes for anticipating change are visioning, sensing, and monitoring.

➤ VISIONING

Visioning is a way of thinking about the future with imagination and wisdom. It is a process for establishing a context for action by crystalizing and communicating your essential aspiration for the organization, how stakeholders contribute to that definition of success, and implicitly with what forces it must contend. Thus, visioning provides a baseline view against which relevant change can be judged and appropriate responses considered. Amazon.com has certainly been one of the truly visionary, transformative, and agile companies. Its vision statement provides clear meaning, power, and aspiration for every stakeholder in the Amazon business model: "...be Earth's most customer-centric company, where customers can find and discover anything they might want to buy online...at the lowest possible prices."

The purpose and utility of visioning is not well understood and is deployed even less effectively. Vision statements are those dusty things that yellow over time in corporate reception areas, right? Agile organizations and leaders recognize the power and energy that come from creating and communicating real clarity. Organizations and their workers need a sense of values, direction, and priorities that guide actions and build the enterprise value proposition. Widespread clarity and understanding of these core elements provide the kind of sense of direction a captain and crew of a sailing vessel derive from having a clear point of sail and compass. The nature and process of creating vision and strategy has to adapt with current VUCA times as planning processes become synchronous, integrated actions and not episodic.

Visioning is an essential capability for anticipating change because it provides the context for understanding what and how forces of change are relevant. Highly visual strategy maps have become an outstanding vehicle for communicating and cascading understanding of the critical elements in the visioning process. The ability to rally collective focus effectively depends on the clarity of the corporate vision message since that message defines what the organization must become agile about. Consider the experience of David Van Eekeren, third generation CEO of Land O'Frost, based just south of Chicago and at the time of this writing, the number two brand of packaged lunchmeats in the U.S. Back in 2008, David had just been named president after more than two decades of progressive apprenticeship learning almost every aspect of the business. If you remember, 2008 was a very turbulent time with the financial tsunami in full force. David and his mother, Donna, then CEO and board chair, knew their business delivered great and important everyday value to families across America and also they knew they needed to invest in growth and innovation to continue their success in the age of power retailers and mega brand competitors.

The Van Eekerens and their Land O'Frost leadership team embarked on a comprehensive journey shaping a fresh, new vision for their company, a vision that codified important elements of their existing company culture combined with new clarity for their strategic roadmap, employee engagement, and the agility imperative. If you were to ask David Van Eekeren what has helped his organization succeed and continue to be the fastest growing brand in its category, his answer would be the power of visioning and actively sharing their strategy map—building a framework for collaboration, engaging the leadership team in shaping the business, and delivers the power of clarity when communicating throughout every level by every echelon of the team.

Visioning can be practiced in many ways, but if it is to be valuable in creating and shaping organizational agility, the following aspects must be made clear:

VISIONING IN AGILITY STRATEGY MAPS

Vision	What is the aspirational statement for why your organization exists?
Stakeholders	Who are the critical stakeholders for your success?
Culture	What core values will shape the culture for how you operate?
Operating Principles	What are the essential operating principles that everyone in the organization should know and understand to be successful? .
Edge	What is the competitive advantage edge that makes you special?
Objectives	What goals will define your success over the next three to five years?
Strategies	What key focus areas define how you will achieve that success?
Metrics	How will you measure and sustain success?

The elements defined here—vision, stakeholders, culture, operating principles, edge, objectives, strategies, and metrics—comprise the basics of the agility strategy map. A clear understanding throughout the organization of each of these elements, in any form of a strategy map, provides a meaningful framework for functional and location teams to and powerful connect to the visioning process and build the framework for alignment connectivity and accountability. As was done in the Land O'Frost case, each location and function must build its own corresponding strategy map in order to build line of sight to their alignment and connectivity. Having a market-right business plan cascaded and vibrant throughout the organization is like creating a central nervous system for sending and receiving vital information and corresponding reflexive action.

Clarity in visioning will not only help your organization build the right framework for evaluating its health and vitality, but also for building organizational support and insight into how it must change to be successful. Questions about "How are we doing?" will not be abstract and rhetorical, but grounded in an aligned framework for evaluating strengths and weaknesses and determining gaps in performance and behaviors. The strategy map framework provides the calibration system for these critical evaluations. Too often organizations go through a perfunctory annual strategic-planning process evaluating traditional SWOT (strengths, weaknesses, opportunities, and threats) assessments in a generic abstract way only to come to bland, innocuous conclusions—a largely worthless exercise. A SWOT analysis based on the visioning inherent in an agility strategy map becomes an extraordinarily useful and impactful exercise.

Significantly more important is an evaluation that begins from a centered viewpoint of three critical questions: *Why* do we exist? *How* will we be successful? *What* does that success look like for our stakeholders? The value proposition for agility is fully integrated when it becomes an inextricable aspect of the delivery system for success. Visioning and the strategy map communication system provide the direction for the journey in a highly visual and digital global culture.

➤ SENSING

Sensing is an early alert system created for the active, comprehensive, and continuous scanning of the organization's internal and external environments. We already know that the VUCA external environment is hyper-turbulent with many unpredictable characteristics. That makes the implications for creating more finely-tuned sensing systems ever more important lest organizations simply operate in "Chicken Little" hysteria, panicking at every vibration.

Society reflects the tendency for panic. In our homes and communities, we have numerous sensing devices such as smoke alarms, carbon dioxide alarms, thermostats, security alarms, and even watch dogs. In our communities, we have local weather news, the Emergency Broadcasting System, tornado sirens, and other systems that provide early warning signals or alerts to changing conditions or impending danger, all helping us stay safer. We can, and must, construct comparable sensing systems for our organizations if we hope to anticipate change and operate as an agile enterprise.

Traditional long-range planning models, with their inward

focus and reliance on historical data, do not encourage decision-makers to anticipate environmental changes and assess the impact of those changes on organizations to the extent needed in this turbulent era. The underlying assumption of such models is that any future change is a continuation of the direction and rate of present trends among a limited number of social, technological, economic, and political variables. Thus, the future for the organization is assumed to reflect the past and present or, in essence, to be surprise-free. However, we know this is not true, and the further we plan into the future, the less it will be true. What is needed now are provisional assumptions that unlock the future from the past, applied through a new planning system of continuous environment sensing, review, and revision tied to an action arm discussed in chapter 7 on initiating action.

As with any sensory-receptor system, effectiveness depends on the design and fine tuning to create a system that can capture and transmit awareness and information that can be received and recognized. In the residential example, your carbon dioxide detector will not make a very effective burglar alarm or motion detector. Building an effective environment sensing system for your enterprise starts with the progressive examination of your strategy map elements to identify the variables and change dynamics that can limit success in each stakeholder avenue. Over time, organizations and leaders become more alert to the nuances in the forces of change, primarily by extending depth of their sensing capabilities.

This is part of the learning agility that progressively makes agile organizations better and faster. It is much like the technique used when teaching teenagers to drive: Don't look only at the car in front of you but be somewhat observant about what is happening to the car in front of that car if you want to more effectively anticipate any change in road dynamics. A full-blown mapping of your forces of change can take on the appearance of molecular chemistry as you identify and explore the interactive relationships in building an eco-system of environmental and competitive activity.

The goal of agile environmental scanning is to alert decision-makers to potentially significant external changes before they crystallize, so that they might have sufficient lead time to sense and respond to the change. Just as with the differentiation between agility and traditional change-management practices, sensing is a process that operates continuously and not simply as an exercise inside a the typical annual strategic planning process.

As the pace and intensity of change accelerates, the sophistication and strategic nature of sensing must keep up. Technological developments and global connectivity have radically enhanced technical capability for sophisticated sensing, from traditional focus groups to online panels and data mining, big data predictive analytics, and other rapidly advancing mobile means of sensing change. Even with the huge amount of information available today, building a tailored information headset via Google Alerts or other means will help you tune in and listen to the stream of passive and active information that comes to you (or others) more easily and more robustly on a daily basis. No longer is it necessary or even feasible to surf the whole wide world of information to stay alert or informed on any topic. Agile organizations and leaders are building sensing systems that stream information and insight to workers that can use all of that in making decisions or initiating action. These sensing systems that are fluid, informed, and proactive. They are part of the systematic way organizations can establish and refine learning agility for individuals and for the organization as a whole.

For many organizations, the fields of customer relationship management and competitive intelligence are primary frontiers for building intimate linkages to ongoing probing and sensing of customer and consumer needs and directions. These fields require continuous improvement and evaluation for determining what is on-target and for understanding when and why organizations miss the boat. If an organization's sensing capabilities are not surfacing relevant trends early enough, it becomes a priority to keep searching to find new angles and avenues.

While mapping the *external* environmental forces of change is paramount, agile organizations must also routinely examine *internal* forces of change and pockets of internal resistance to necessary change. The goal is to create an adaptive and nimble organization that is able to respond horizontally across functions and silos to delight stakeholders and end customers whose needs continuously change, thus requiring the organization to build and embrace a continuously adaptive response capability.

➤ MONITORING

Monitoring is a process for systematically tracking organizational and selected environmental activities and their effects to help leaders recognize and interpret trends and patterns better and faster. There are so many moving parts in today's new-age economy that create a universe of complexity for business leaders to sort through in making sense of their businesses. This is where the ability to anticipate change is built through real-time alignment of sensing capabilities that feed a monitoring capability focused on tracking leading indicators to identify key patterns and trends. Identifying these trends early in the game facilitates communication regarding updated awareness and insights swiftly and directly to those responsible for taking appropriate action. Monitoring for the sake of monitoring is the business of historians and statisticians. Agile organizations, on the other hand, are built to take appropriate action as they construct and use their sensing and monitoring capabilities to help quickly adapt to adversity and seize opportunities.

The corporate scrapyard is full of organizations that were caught off guard with sudden changes in consumer preferences, shifts in key customer strategies, unexpected technology or competitor leaps. The corporate speed of play is accelerating and requires organizations to sense and respond better and faster every day. Agile organizations determine the right key performance indicators to help their leaders rapidly recognize important patterns and trends affecting business success. Increasingly, these leaders are depending on business analytics and dashboards to help them monitor and interpret the universe of complexity they face—in real time. We believe there is a whole category of important forward looking indicators to monitor called Key Agility Indicators.

Other important forces of change involve monitoring external stakeholders, especially consumers, customers, suppliers, and competitors. Successful agile organizations have established ongoing monitoring capabilities, sometimes involving external resources, to help them educate and inform their strategies and operating dexterity with the insight they gain from that monitoring. The incredible access to mobile technology and the exploding field of mobile device apps enables greater use and integration of smart technologies to improve and speed decision-making because key factors are better monitored and trend information is more readily available.

➤ TIPS TO HELP YOU ANTICIPATE CHANGE

1. Create a one-page strategy map that captures the critical success factors embodied in your vision-to-action plan.

2. Build an environmental scan that includes all the stakeholders in your success model detailing the primary forces of change that can disrupt that success.

3. Determine the key trends happening for each of these forces of change along with the implications of those trends.

4. Determine how you will monitor those trends.

CHAPTER 6

G is for Generating Confidence

Confidence is something that seems to be in short supply these days, across our country and the rest of the world. Remember when elected leaders and major financial institutions actually engendered high trust and confidence? We now live in an era where our confidence and trust in elected leaders and major institutions are at an all-time low. The volatility and uncertainty we face each day erodes our sense of confidence. Research clearly shows that confidence is strongly linked to individual, team, organizational, and even national productivity and sense of well-being. In our hyper-turbulent world, it is amazing how fast confidence can crash but also, with the power of social networking, how fast it can grow. Increasing confidence is a significant goal of many efforts to improve organizational climate and culture. But climate and culture efforts sometimes seem so large and complex that attempting to address these broad scale and institutional issues feels like a futile proposition. We believe that generating confidence with all stakeholders is a direct and comprehensible goal worthy of systematic effort of action and measurement. Truly agile organizations have a total stakeholder orientation that includes customers, suppliers, consumers, communities, owners and even regulators too.

Confidence is one of those hard-to-measure, yet extraordinarily important, dynamics. Just rewind your memory over the past few years to find a world full of examples of lost confidence—consumer confidence, corporate uncertainties, geopolitical and societal disillusionment. From these examples and more, you can see the impact that lost confidence has on the economic well-being and attitudes of whole countries, corporations, regions, and individuals.

Confidence within organizations can be positively affected by managing three essential processes: connecting, aligning, and engaging. Successful development of these processes enables the growth of internal confidence that flows through to all stakeholders. Building a high confidence coefficient with all stakeholders is an excellent agile enterprise success measure.

➤ CONNECTING

Connecting is a process for bringing people together by making sure each stakeholder understands how his or her work or role contributes to the organization's mission as well as how the work of others contributes to its mission.

There are special leaders who have a powerful capability to create these connections to the organization's purpose and goals that goes beyond pure information sharing and reaches into the emotional cortex where commitment lives. People want to be connected—to the organization's purpose and vision as well as to each other. When they are connected, they feel inspired.

One of the classic stories about connecting an individual with an overall enterprise objective happened in 1961 when President John F. Kennedy declared in his State of the Union speech that America should "commit itself to achieving the goal, before this decade is out, of landing a man on the moon and returning him safely to the earth." Soon after, JFK was reported to have visited NASA and spoken with a janitor, asking him about what his job involved. "My job," said the NASA janitor, "is to help put a man on the moon." That is a great example of an individual who became truly connected to the ultimate mission of the organization.

You can imagine the transformative sense of pride and purpose that results as organization members personally connect their roles and identify with the purpose and enterprise objective. Organizations and leaders that are able to create this profound connection are somewhat like modern devices making a Bluetooth connection. You know that you have connected these devices because the blue light illuminates indicating that a solid connection has been made and communication can now happen. Outstanding leaders like JFK or Martin Luther King have extraordinary ability to create that Bluetooth-like connectivity that results in passion and commitment.

Leaders who are building connection also find ways to make organizational goals relevant to all the people in the organization. A line of sight needs to be clear for how each person contributes to the organization's success and why it is worthwhile for everyone to strive for success in the first place. Simon Sinek, a fresh voice and author who has gained widespread awareness from his powerful TED talks, provides several good lessons in his recent books *Start with Why* and *Leaders Eat Last*, emphasizing how many great leaders inspire others by being exceedingly intentional in connecting. Leaders who connect at the *why* level more effectively build loyalty and commitment. Those leaders who tend to operate at the *what* level create a purely transactional climate where workers are merely doing a job and moving from one sometimes menial task to another.

Agile leaders do an equally good job at bringing that same VIP sensation to all stakeholder relationships, including external customers and suppliers, invigorating a strong sense of connection with a shared sense of mutual success. Agile leaders behave in noticeably different ways from other leaders and the conversation they promote is likewise different. Agile leaders regularly check in with team members to reinforce and affirm the value they see in each team member's contribution for the team. Regular infusions of this kind of positive dynamism keep the central nervous system across the organization energized and informed on exactly *how* what each person does contributes to overall organizational success. There are many valuable bi-products from this kind of leadership, especially the climate-setting tone for active two-way communication and feedback, which provides the best sensing system available—fully connected and active dialogue up and down organizational lines.

➤ ALIGNING

Aligning is the process of matching up organizational vision, values, and goals in line with stakeholder priorities, actions, energy, and time allocations. It must be a continuous process where leaders learn from both successes and failures, and it requires constant effort. This is where the growing complexity and ambiguity in the world makes things increasingly difficult. Faced with competing priorities and realities that challenge organization ethics and values, often across geographies and cultures, leaders today often find their efforts to stay completely aligned exhausting. Just as with automobiles, when things get out of alignment, the ride starts getting bumpy and the wear and tear factor on all the moving parts gets stressed.

Leadership's strategic alignment must be supported with some simple yet profound processes that help translate vision to action, much like a driveshaft transfers potential energy from a car engine into real traction. The success or failure of leadership's alignment efforts translates directly into how well the organization executes against its priorities. When things that are deemed truly important actually get the primary focus and resources, alignments are reinforced and corporate confidence is built.

From our experience and research, we find that organizations, through active alignment and conversation flow, maintain active strategic focus and dialogue on mission-critical projects at each level of the enterprise and thereby produce better and faster mission-critical outcomes. This continuous focusing and calibration process is a central feature of agile organizations; they must stay focused first before they can be fast and flexible at capabilities that ultimately matter. The capability is much like the auto-focus on most cameras adjusting and bringing clarity as the landscape changes. High performance cameras have high speed lens and action settings designed to bring focus even with fast motion. High performance organizations will build out comparable capabilities to create focus as the speed of business continues to accelerate.

The right timing for your continuous alignment and planning process will be a function of variables in your industry and competitive environment; it could be annual, bi-annual, or quarterly. In chaotically turbulent environments, it may need to be monthly or even weekly. Traditional models of laborious strategic planning spanning months or more have given way to a variety of alternative fast-strategy methods.

Often ignored, leadership behavior—the daily walk of the talk—is a critically important element in how alignment impacts an organization's confidence, customer relationships, and shareholder value. Agile organizations create and communicate clear codes of conduct for its leaders, employees, and all stakeholders. The greater the variability of real behavior to the code, the more drag develops, preventing the organization from becoming truly aerodynamic. To generate confidence in organizations, alignment has to first start within each leader.

Mahatma Gandhi had a brilliant framework for understanding this notion of alignment in his definition of true happiness. For Gandhi, true "Happiness is when what you think, what you say, and what you do are all in harmony." The same goal can exist for organizations because its vision, values, and priorities represent what it thinks; leadership conversation and communication represent what it says; and leadership actions represent what it does.

Do you have alignment in your organization? If you do, you will have a better chance of being focused, fast, and flexible.

➤ ENGAGING

Engaging is the process of building commitment to what the organization is doing, trusting that actions are in accordance with values, and being aware that everyone's contribution is invited and appreciated.

Your organization's success depends increasingly on an engaged workforce that benefits from meaningful work it can claim and a clear organizational direction. The engaged and agile workforce operates in an organizational culture characterized by curiosity, caring, connecting, committing, challenging, and creating. Each of these characteristics helps build the texture for a high-engagement culture that reinforces one of your core beliefs: Make your people your priority and you will supercharge your journey to agility.

Successful organizations capitalize on the diverse backgrounds, knowledge, skills, creativity, and motivation of their workforce and partners. Truly valuing the organization's people means committing to their on-going engagement, satisfaction, development, and well-being. Increasingly, this involves more flexible, high-performance work practices tailored to varying workplace and home-life needs. Creating a fully engaged workforce is not an easy undertaking, particularly in these somewhat cynical times when continuing trust is under continuous stress from economic crises, multigenerational and cultural dynamics, and a myriad of other issues adding extra complexity. Currently, corporate engagement is declining, but the payoff of an engaged workforce is huge, as studies have shown that highly engaged teams outperform average teams by more than three times. Organizations have few other productivity levers nearly this potent. The key is tapping into the 40 percent of their discretionary effort reserved for when they feel valued and engaged. This is the 40 percent premium for real leadership.

An important aspect of building a high-engagement climate has to do with building skills and capabilities for success within the workforce. Increasingly, workers today are motivated in environments where they can bring their skills and expertise to add value, doing work that provides meaning and purpose for them within their view of the world. Organizations that actually believe that their people truly are the most important asset will find ways to encourage and invest in developing their people's talents.

Connecting, aligning, and engaging are the organizational processes for generating confidence; leadership communication is the vehicle for making it happen. In this era of information overload, there is an abundance of noise and clutter that distorts leadership messaging within most organizations. A few years ago the American Management Association conducted a study on strategy execution that highlighted key factors differentiating organizations that execute strategy successfully from those who did not. A major differentiation exists in those firms that worked hard to create clarity of message throughout their organizations. One of our client organization's was able to bring clarity of its message throughout its organization via the development and deployment of a clear strategy map broadcasting on their internal TV channel found in all company break rooms as well as aligning in its company profit sharing plan. More importantly, the conversation changed and clarity increased. Mike Richardson, one of our ACT principals, likes to remind us that it is the "conversation flow that leads to cash flow."

Confidence is about being most capable and prepared for winning, which leads to optimism, a strong desire to succeed, and a high level of effort and risk-taking. On the other hand, a lack of confidence results in pessimism, a sense of futility, half-hearted effort, denial, fear of risk-taking, and ongoing frustration. Many business leaders are struggling with ways to generate confidence in their workforces. Right now the number one issue eroding confidence is uncertainty. It's almost better to get bad news rather than no news, so at least people know and can begin planning accordingly.

A high level of employee confidence is achieved when employees perceive their organization is being effectively managed with good business processes and competitively positioned with attractive products. They believe they have a promising future within their organization, true job security, and enhanced skills that would be attractive to other employers outside their organization. Confidence is bolstered in organizations with healthy resilience and the capability of bouncing back from adversity or failure. It's not possible to win every customer competition, delight consumers with each promotional campaign, or create new category leaders with every new product launch. Failure is inevitable, and part of the ability to keep teams engaged depends on how your organization responds to adversity. More specifically, it comes down to how you and other leaders respond and react during challenging times.

Confidence is built as employees see the company leaders living by the organization's vision and values, by aligning employees with the organization's business goals, maintaining a candid dialogue with employees, recognizing employees' contributions and progress, and creating an inclusive and caring environment.

➤ TIPS TO HELP YOU GENERATE CONFIDENCE

1. Make sure your organization has clear, communicated goals that connect and engage everyone with a sense of shared responsibility.

2. Have your teams meet and identify those things that help and those things that are obstacles to team success; have them a conduct a continue-start-and-stop (CSS) discussion to build some action plans to enhance alignment and understanding. In a CSS discussion, share those things that you value about each other that you hope will continue; share suggestions that you ask others to consider start doing; and share suggestions you would like others

to consider stop doing to improve the effectiveness of relationships and team outcomes.

3. Build engagement by promoting a monthly team what's-happening communication gathering: a stand-up thirty-minute session to promote communication and engagement.

CHAPTER 7

I is for Initiating Action

Why is improving an organization's capability for initiating action so important today? Growing complexity is one reason, which, when combined with the pace of business today, is creating an environment where only the fittest survive.

This growing pace and complexity will continue to bring extraordinary stress and pressure on the leadership system for most organizations and will be increasingly destructive for those organizations and leaders that continue to try and use hierarchical, command-and-control decision-making and management practices. Similarly, those organizations whose leaders continue to resist adopting the latest technology, including social-networking-based tools increasingly used to enhance and speed action and collaboration across organizations, will likewise end up missing in action. Although this growing complexity and pace creates challenges for all and fatalities for some, it also creates a great opportunity for differentiation and competitive advantage. Leaders who are able to build superior skill in sensing and responding better and faster, especially in developing high-performance collaborative teams talented in those skills, will be creating real, sustainable advantages for success and personal growth.

What are the essentials for creating organizations that initiate action on a world-class basis? The total compression equation (time multiplied by complexity multiplied by rising expectations) puts a premium on organizations that can operate with a great sense of urgency; disciplined decision-making enabled down through the organization; and widespread, active collaboration viewed as a competitive advantage factor.

These are the three key processes for building an action-oriented organization that include creating bias for action, improving widespread decision-making capabilities, and building skill in active collaboration.

Organizations focused on getting better and faster at these three processes for action have the best chance of keeping up with the pace of change and complexity.

➤ CREATING A BIAS FOR ACTION

Creating a bias for action is the process for instilling a shared inclination to act—and a true sense of urgency about it—with all organizational members. *Bias* is a word that is too often meant in a pejorative sense. However, it can refer to an inclination or prejudice in favor or against a particular person or thing. But bias, as used in this book, simply means an inclination towards something—in this case, action. Agile organizations have a fundamentally different attitude about making things—the right things— happen. Agile organizations are designed to continuously ratchet their performance and capabilities higher without needing to be told to do so by owners or customers; it's an inherent trait. They are also characterized by a positive determination and commitment to action reminiscent of the children's video, *Bob the Builder*, watched and mimicked by young children who walk about their houses calling out, "Can we do it? Yes, we can!"

John Kotter, Harvard professor and recognized thought leader on the dynamics of organizational change, characterizes three types of organizations in his book entitled, *A Sense of Urgency*: organizations that are complacent, organizations with a false sense of urgency, and organizations with a *true* sense of urgency.

- **The organization that is complacent** may have had a history of success, may have been an industry leader, and still expects to continue in that same anointed position. These organizations do not recognize their significance slipping or reduced competitiveness until it is often too late. They may have had an important competitive advantage at one point in time, but as the pace and dynamics of change accelerate, some competitive advantages dissipate or even disappear.

- **Organizations with a false sense of urgency** project much frenetic activity from constant meetings and conference calls often filled with tension and conflict between from silo-hardened team members who lob corporate grenades believing the enemy may live within the company compound. Everyone here seems to believe there is a sense of urgency because they all leave exhausted every day but accomplish relatively little.

- **The organization with a true sense of urgency**, by contrast, is one with almost comparable amount of hyper-frenetic activity but with an altogether different feeling about it. This organization is purpose-driven, aligned, and operates with a strong values-based code of conduct that enables and encourages positive action, expecting team members to demonstrate unconditional respect up and down the ranks. Here everyone is expected to act as a leader highly engaged and committed to the team mission and success. There is a uniformity of expectation—the bias for action does not just live in senior leadership veins; everyone is included in the adventure of making important things happen. Agile organizations have such a true sense of urgency.

Over the past several years, we have been working with leaders of a very large consumer products company to help them identify ways to increase organizational agility and speed of action. They had experienced several years of significant turbulence and serial reorganization chaos as they spun off from their mega-size parent company. The CEO made sure there was a great deal of formal communication and messaging about action and priorities, but organizational responsiveness was still seriously lacking. After a series of interviews with most of the organization's senior leaders, one contributing factor to the near-paralysis this organization was facing became clear.

The CEO had created a weekly management meeting protocol that was initially designed to bring greater focus and urgency for getting turnaround on key performance factors. But it actually had the effect of clogging up the action and decision-making arteries. The weekly agenda became increasingly tactical, getting into detailed issues surrounding supply chain bottlenecks or forecasting glitches and methods. The protocol caused the senior most leaders in this multibillion dollar organization to decide they each needed to be fully armed with detailed status information for any range of questions that were routinely tossed out by the CEO's earnest effort to cut through red tape and solve things.

It took several days prior to each weekly meeting to get ready (which, since the meeting was held on Mondays, meant those prior days routinely involved preparing over every weekend). Of course, each of the department heads had their teams engaged in report generation to make sure each senior executive was armed with answers for questions that invariably dealt with things that had already happened rather than leveraging the executive talent and focus to look forward. The mantra or poster needed in many executive conference rooms is, "Lead more and manage less."

The key to creating a true bias for action comes down to setting the tone and expectations for how the organization operates, including how individual senior leaders model that behavior along with great clarity about the organization's goals and priorities. In the absence of these factors, organizations stall and can become like the deer in the headlights as the blur of business occurs.

How do you know whether your organization has a sense of urgency or bias for action? Here are a few questions to ask and explore:

- What is the meeting purpose and protocol you have established? Do you have weekly, bi-weekly, monthly, and quarterly meetings?

- Are you flying at the right altitude in your meetings, or are you creating meetings for inspection purposes? Whose job is that kind of inspection anyway? Are you leading or managing?

- What drives your agendas and determines your priorities? Are your agenda and priorities related to accomplishing mission-critical goals or just issues that come up day to day?

- Do your teams tend to keep talking about the same issues, or do they come to conclusions and determine courses of action to follow?

- When teams decide a course of action, do they establish clear, expected due dates and action from owners who have full accountability for results?

- How long are the meetings that you and your teams routinely have? Are they excessive and painful, or crisp and focused?

➤ DECISION-MAKING FOR A NEW AGE

How you make decisions can either be the crux of accomplishment or the agony of complacency, if not done with quality, speed, and depth of understanding in its important role in an agile organization. Improving decision-making is a process ensuring that solving problems and choosing appropriate actions to take are done efficiently and quickly, and are distributed throughout the organization horizontally and vertically.

Speed of action is often limited by the speed of decision-making. In many organizations, the slowest cycle time is management's decision-making. A recent study by the research arm of *The Economist* journal identified slow decision-making and existence of silos within the organization as two of the key constraints to being able to remain competitive in today's fast-paced race for success. This is due in part to the rapidly increasing level of complexity that burdens and slows the decision-making process, and also because the slowdown takes more of the limited time available to make these decisions. Business is operating in a world with only one time zone: *now*. We have a growing intolerance for waiting for anything, especially decisions. Yet there are risks in many decisions with sometimes unclear consequences, both personal and corporate.

Imagine for a moment that you are like that NASCAR driver zooming around the business track at nearly 200 mph, weaving in and out of cross-functional collisions and customer-driven near misses. Suddenly you realize that it is the track that is moving at high speed and even when you take your foot off the accelerator, things don't really slow down that much—you just have less control over the steering. Your decision-making pace and effectiveness comprise one of the key factors determining the speed at which you can move your organization forward. It also contributes greatly to your sense of confidence and leadership composure.

Anyone who has played fluid, free-flowing sports like basketball, soccer, lacrosse, or ice hockey at higher competitive levels can attest that one of the most profound differences between the higher competitor and more recreational amateur level is the speed of play. The game just gets faster and faster as the competition level rises. Consequently, the skill level of players must increase at a comparable rate or they become ineffective or obsolete— and end up on the bench. Anticipation, decision-making, and creativity must all flow naturally at the stepped-up pace in order to compete effectively at the higher levels. The same scenarios apply to business organizations.

From our work and research, we've determined the three keys for enhancing decision-making speed and effectiveness relate to: improving clarity on decision rights; mitigating fear and consequences of decision-making failure; and, most importantly, adopting and effectively using more disciplined tools to enhance decision-making quality. The use of disciplined tools like those we introduce in coming pages are a major factor that helps enable leaders to push decision-making down to lower levels in the organization.

Decision rights are often a causality of organizational turbulence and disorientation. There may have been a point in time when it was clear to everyone who had the right to make which decisions. That may have been when the business processes were first established and the first team was trained within an organization. Then along came reorganization to a matrixed structure, followed by three more rounds of downsizing or rightsizing over a three- to five-year period. That is actually a pretty mild description of typical organizational behavior in this age compared to what some organizations driven by high growth via acquisition or merger experience. Consider previous organization dynamics and it's no wonder that ambiguity and confusion over decision rights continue to handicap most organizations. Ensuring role clarity and rebooting the decision matrix each time major change happens is an absolute requirement for agile leaders and teams today.

Mitigating fear and negative consequences is the second key factor inhibiting decision speed. We were conducting a team development workshop in Virginia a few years ago to help a newly-arrived manager overcome and repair some early-days' potholes in team relationships. The team was working diligently in small groups identifying the obstacles that kept them from becoming what in an earlier exercise they had determined to be their ideal agile team. Each team then built their obstacles discussion into a creative collage using magazine cutouts to help tell their stories. One of the teams had held a robust discussion and bravely included an image representing the fear factor as one of their key obstacles. We had coached the manager in advance that there might be the potential for some awkward, candid conversations during the workshop and in fact that would be a good sign if it happened. That moment led to some very open, constructive discussion about what the team was feeling and how they had interpreted some of the manager's behaviors. The new manager was earnestly interested in being an effective leader but had been so focused on trying to figure out turnaround solutions on his own that he inadvertently alienated his team and created a climate of fear that nearly paralyzed the entire unit.

Heightened fear and anxiety are often by-products of today's turbulent world and can impact decision speed from just slowing things down to total paralysis due to fear of making decisions without the boss's involvement. Clarifying decision rights helps minimize the organizational reluctance that comes from the fear factor but that underlying tension from fear is most directly controlled by the climate set by the leader. Procter & Gamble's Chairman of the Board, President, and CEO A. G. Lafley promotes the notion that failure is just another word for learning and recognizes that if he has widespread fear of failure operating in his organization, it is unlikely he will be able to foster the kind of crisp decision-making and innovation that he knows is required for success in a highly competitive global marketplace.

Disciplined tools are critical to the agile organization. It's common to hear the shout for more employee empowerment and involvement in workplace decisions, but when push comes to shove it usually doesn't happen. Pushing decision rights to the lowest capable level can be a direct accelerator for speed of action, but it relies on an effective process for building competency at ever lower levels in the organization. Stephen M. R. Covey identifies in his book *The Speed of Trust* that trust has two major components: character and competence. Determining whether the character or integrity of an individual to do the right thing and if the individual has the competence, skills, and experience to do the job right are critical in fostering trust. Those two major factors determine whether organizations are able to effectively push decision-making down in their hierarchy. Management is more likely to relinquish decision-making authority and responsibility when these two conditions are positively satisfied—the right people of character with the competence and track record to own and be accountable for making a range of decisions. Building competence in better and faster decisions is a skill that can be developed. Aligning rapid decision-making throughout the organization grounded in a clear understanding of the enterprise core value equation where each individual is adding special value is a critical part of the equation for sustainability of success and making agility a competitive advantage.

One of the real challenges leaders face in the ever-increasing speed and complexity of business today is the temptation to make all the decisions. There are natural forces and tensions that can make the centripetal tendency towards leadership control over decisions attractive. In the end, that approach ends up slowing down the enterprise compared to its potential decision speed that can be realized if leaders build competence, skill, and capacity for better and faster decisions throughout the organization. It is much like the difference in computer processing speeds that have evolved over the past decade. Many remember the old 286k processors in early generations of computers that would be totally incapable of processing today's average daily computer content. The latest generations of processors are radically faster and more capable than the 286 generation. This differential is reflective of the kind of evolution that must also take place in our organizational processors—the processors also known as people.

Here's a description of the decision-making and problem-solving method we promote and teach our clients, called the OODA LOOP (OODA stands for Observe, Orient,

Decide, Act and LOOP stands for Locating, Orienting, Operating, Perpetuating) system. It was originated by Colonel John Boyd, an air force pilot during the Korean War who helped United Nations forces overcome considerable disadvantage against the North Koreans in terms of number and newness of combat aircraft. Boyd's focus on rapid decision capability helped identify and exploit a tactical limitation in the enemy aircraft and strategy. This factor became a breakthrough in the air battle and progressively changed the dynamics including the morale and confidence of pilots on the U.S. and United Nations side. The keys to Boyd's OODA model comes from the iterative and rapid calibration and recalibration steps especially throughout the Observe and Orient steps. Observe and Orient are what we consider the strategic thinking perspectives built into this decision process and represent often overlooked or minimized steps in today's usual and customary approach to decision-making by many leaders. All too often, we see the ready-fire-aim approach enacted. Agile leaders can help create poise and composure during even chaotic times by helping asking the Observe and Orient kind of questions to help ground the problem-solving process—even in the midst of crisis.

We added the strategic and tactical callouts in our work using the OODA LOOP about ten years ago when working with a group of high potential leaders in an accelerated leadership session on strategic agility. One of the bright young leaders attending asked a great question—"What does it mean to be more strategic?" His manager told the young leader that he wanted him to become more strategic, and he earnestly wanted to understand what he would or should be doing to be more strategic. It led to a rich discussion about strategic and tactical behavior.

The OODA model provides a very good framework for understanding strategic and tactical behavior. The Observe and Orient steps provide the strategic landscaping that enables more focused Decide and Act to create the solutions and traction for success. We built this basic model as a starter wizard to help leaders and teams begin to approach problems or decisions that need solutions. Introducing and building awareness and use with the OODA Loop within organizations is a great way to build meaningful capability that will build confidence, grow engagement and help leaders progressively delegate and empower their teams. Building widespread skill and confidence in good decision making is one of the high-payback initiatives any leader can implement. Obviously there are numerous residual benefits from such an investment: it increases the speed, accountability, responsiveness and overall confidence of your people to see themselves as effective "solutions providers" in every function, especially for customer-facing team members.

How do you know if your current decision-making process and capability are agile enough for today's speed of play? Here are a few questions you can ask and explore.

- Do you work on the same issues over and over again,

OODA PROBLEM-SOLVING SYSTEM

STRATEGIC THINKING	OBSERVE	• What is the real problem statement we are trying to solve?
		• Describe the current state of the problem.
		• What facts do we have about the problem?
		• Is it getting better or getting worse? What is the momentum?
		• What do we need to know that we don't know about the problem?
		• Who are the critical stakeholders in the problem outcome?
	ORIENT	• What does the desired state for this problem look like?
		• What are the gaps between what we want and where we are?
		• How do the gaps relate to other stakeholder interests?
		• What are the benefits for creating the desired outcome?
		• What are the obstacles to the desired outcome?
		• Are there differences in stakeholder motivation, values, or biases?
TACTICAL THINKING	DECIDE	• What are our alternative courses of action that we could take?
		• How does each deliver on our desired outcome, achieve benefit, and overcome obstacles?
		• What are the criteria we use for making the right decisions?
		• Who should be included in the idea generation process?
		• How do the possible alternative actions satisfy other stakeholder needs?
		• Based on this consideration, what is the right course of action?
	ACT	• How should we implement the recommended solution—change management implications?
		• What is the best communication and feedback approach to key stakeholders?
		• What will be the critical milestones to insure successful implementation?
		• What will be our measure of success for solving this issue?
		• What will be the follow-up measure and frequency to monitor success?
		• How can we do this process better next time?

addressing just the surface and not getting to the root causes of the problem?

- When your people come visit you in your office, are they bringing you problems so you can give the answers or do they bring well-thought-out recommended solutions to these issues?

- Does everyone in your organization tend to say, "I have to go check with my boss"?

➤ COLLABORATING

Collaborating is a process for building the capability of people to work together across boundaries (functional, hierarchical, geographical, and more). By setting focused expectations and developing a range of interpersonal skills associated with enhancing communications, team problem-solving, influencing, and conflict management styles, collaborating teams are supported in creating and implementing important solutions. Collaboration is much more than just a nice idea. It is a major opportunity area for serious competitive advantage, reserved for those who truly invest in the concept and its associated capability building. This advantage will become increasingly clear and essential as time advances.

Our work includes supporting a well-known global consumer brand in building its collaboration capability of key in-country leaders by providing coaching services on decision-making, influencing, conflict management, and leadership communication aligned with their strategy focus. Striving to build a shared global consciousness around strategic imperatives, they also focused on building the essential skills that leaders who are expected to advance in the organization and gain additional responsibility must have for success, especially in highly-matrixed global teams where much collaboration is done virtually.

Most organizations today recognize the extraordinary power that is available by promoting active collaboration but often get distracted by and mired in the complexity and turbulence of daily operations. *Working Beyond Borders* is a 2010 IBM study of seven hundred chief human resource officers from across the globe. The study found three key workforce gaps as the biggest opportunities for the human resource function of the future:

1. Cultivating creative leaders who can more nimbly lead in complex, global environments.

2. Mobilizing for greater speed and flexibility, producing significantly greater capability to adjust underlying costs and faster ways to allocate talent.

3. Capitalizing on collective intelligence through much more effective collaboration across increasingly global teams.

The message remains clear and consistent: Future success demands greater creativity, speed, and flexibility in how our organizations operate, leveraging those who have the skills to bring out the best from increasingly diverse and often remote teams.

Collaboration must be critically important because companies such as Cisco Systems and Citrix introduced sixty-one new technologies during 2009 alone—all focused on capturing a greater share of what is now a fifty-billion-dollar, rapidly growing collaboration technology market, a market that is estimated to exceed seventy-five billion dollars in 2017. For there to be that much new market size created in the course of only about three years, means that many recognize that building; collaboration capability is a significant leverage factor moving forward.

In fact, collaboration and innovation may be the key organizational skills to differentiate success in the twenty-first century. Collaboration has often been viewed as an attitude, whereas now considering the speed and complexity in most large matrix organizations, collaboration must be actively developed as an integral operating system complete with prerequisite competencies in communications, listening, and process disciplines, as well as interpersonal-relationship-building qualities. There is an emerging art form in the advanced collaboration and leadership skills needed for organizations operating in virtual and global space.

The interconnectedness needed to operate real-time global teams requires communication, collaboration, and engagement to occur via conference call or preferably video conference, Skype or FaceTime as a primary mode of interaction. It can be challenging to build trust, understanding, and commitment with teams that operate at the same location with face-to-face opportunities. Effective global leaders have learned the importance of building human-to-human connectivity and accommodations in the engagement process that recognize and respect the cultural diversity of their team members.

Paradoxically, collaboration is actually getting both harder and easier all the time. Collaboration is getting harder because of the speed of play. It never seems there is enough time to get other people involved in finding solutions even when doing so will improve the outcome. Conflicting functional priorities and measures of success add even more complexity to the collaboration equation.

On the other hand, collaboration is getting easier due to the many amazing technology tools to facilitate the process and productivity, including ShareFile, SharePoint, GoToMeeting, Join.me, Zoom, Trello, and many other often free, open-source tools that support both active and passive collaboration. Passive collaboration is the opportunity to benefit from others' ideas and insights without personal contact via YouTube, LinkedIn, SlideShare, etc.

Collaboration can be a nice and polite word that suggests a collegial climate of considerate, communal feel-good warmth, or it can come to mean something much more strategic, and profound—the intended sense and meaning discussed in the notion of collaborating. Collaboration is intentional, planful, active, and skillful, not meandering, passive, or random.

Organizations need to reexamine the architectural specifications of their simple matrixed organizations and recognize the many dynamics of twenty-first century collaboration that can become dysfunctional if expectations, behaviors, and operating systems used aren't updated. A matrixed team structure can be illustrated by the following figure where projects can also be regions, channels, or other frameworks in your portfolio.

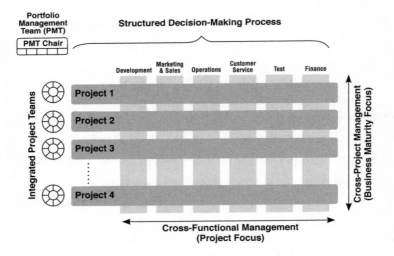

The Agile Model and its associated key processes provide an effective upgrade to most conventional matrix organizations. What follows are some considerations for applying The Agile Model to enhance collaboration and effectiveness in such matrixed organizations today.

OBSERVATIONS FOR MATRIX TEAMS IN BUILDING COLLABORATIVE AGILITY

ANTICIPATE CHANGE	• Complexity and continuous change are major factors facing matrix team success today. How do we learn to adapt? • Are there clarity and focus in the charter scope and expectations set forth for each team? • How good are team processes and practices for sensing and monitoring internal and external forces of change impacting success? • Has each team built skill and insight via scenario planning as a routine planning process?
GENERATE CONFIDENCE	• Is the overall team charter/mission linked to the enterprise strategy map and deployment of strategic imperatives? • Do team members feel and exhibit high levels of connectivity? • Are team rules of engagement and actual behaviors aligned? Are priorities, resources, time, and energy aligned? • Do team members feel emotionally connected and encouraged to provide discretionary effort—and do they?
INITIATE ACTION	• Does the team operate with a sense of urgency? • Is decision-making swift, yet rigorous, and encouraged to be made at the lowest possible level, or is it hoarded at senior levels? • Is there collaboration lip service or true, active, and intentional effort to promote and improve collaboration?

LIBERATE THINKING	• Does the team operate with a sense of urgency? • Is decision-making swift, yet rigorous, and encouraged to be made at the lowest possible level, or is it hoarded at senior levels? • Is there collaboration lip service or true, active, and intentional effort to promote and improve idea generation and collaboration? • Is there a climate encouraging fresh innovative thinking or a cloud of fear shadowing open discourse, thus limiting ideas? • Are internal and external customers actively involved in the idea and creative process—looking beyond today?
EVALUATE RESULTS	• Do we invite, encourage, recognize, and use ideas generated from all areas and levels in and out of the organization? • How well do leaders and teams define expected outcomes and build a culture for accountability, managing by the commitments made to stakeholders and team members? • Do teams have and utilize ways to get and give real-time feedback to/from our teammates, customers, suppliers, etc.? • Do teams have dashboards that define and track critical success factors?

➤ TIPS TO HELP YOU INITIATE ACTION

1. Clarify and confirm the three mission-critical priorities for each function, location, and team member. What is the desired outcome? By when? How will you measure success?

2. Have each team member pick a mission-critical obstacle and initiate a project team, utilizing the OODA problem-solving discipline, to build an improvement plan.

3. Have each functional team leader initiate an exercise to map the internal stakeholders in their success and then rate the quality of each relationship. Afterward, select the lowest rated relationship and initiate a cross-functional team effort to build a game plan to improve positive collaboration using the OODA methodology.

CHAPTER 8

L is for Liberating Thinking

With all the attention that the theory of evolution in biology has received since 1859, especially in recent years, it's easy to forget that evolution is a concept that has been around for centuries. It carries different meanings in different circles, but it normally suggests a gradual transformation. Society has always operated in an evolutionary mode. Lately, however, evolution may be more accurately described by the addition of the letter *r* in front of the word. Yes, revolution is more descriptive of the pace of change for the years to come. That pace of change feeds off of itself as new technology enables even more new possibilities.

Ask anyone who has been responsible for running a business supplying consumer products to retailers and they'll tell you that you had better be inventing your next innovation even before you've launched your latest innovation on the retail floor. Retailers and consumers have an insatiable appetite for newer, better products, generally at lower prices, with a better carbon footprint and more features than before. How can businesses survive with this aggressive expectation for continuous change and reinvention? Perhaps the more important question is how you'll survive if you don't create the culture and expectation in your organization for this kind of fresh, innovative thinking (FIT). The world has indeed become flat with new ideas and better products coming from all corners of the world faster than ever. It is a matter of fitness, and just as in the Olympics, those with the greatest skills related to the critical events will emerge as the world champions.

Thinking is the most common organizational activity. Everyone is thinking all of the time, although it can seem as if they aren't, because thinking often becomes automatic, traditional, and unimaginative. In order to liberate thinking, there are three critical processes: creating a bias for innovation, focusing on customers, and encouraging idea diversity.

➤ CREATING A BIAS FOR INNOVATION

Creating a bias for innovation is a process for making sure that all the stakeholders involved with the organization are open and looking for new ideas about what is being done, what sould be done next, and how to do it better and faster.

For the past dozen years, we have worked to introduce agility across the globe to many thousands of leaders in a variety of organizations with a wide spectrum of managerial roles and levels. One of the exercises we use in introducing how to liberate thinking is conducted in small subgroups. Each subgroup is provided resources in a Ziploc bag (resources might include, for example, Popsicle sticks, rubber bands, glue, tissue paper, and pipe cleaners) and asked to construct an object that represents what their organization might look like if it were the most agile enterprise, highlighting the key characteristics that would make it so.

It is always a pleasure to experience adults working together to create something from resources that are more frequently used by their kids. However, the most distinctive by-product of this exercise is that teams compete against one another instead of combining resources to achieve a better result. Only once in the last ten years have any of the groups combined subgroups to achieve the objective. How often does this internal competition occur within your own organization? Are organizations missing their potential by operating with a paradigm that reflects internal competition for resources versus organizational boundary-spanning agility that reaps the benefits of working collaboratively? How does this silo mentality limit the full potential of liberated thinking and place an arbitrary upper boundary on your organization's agility?

Our concept of liberated thinking is partially defined by the concepts of creativity and innovation. However, liberated thinking is more expansive and greatly dependent on an organization's culture and leadership. What is your leadership doing to instill a culture that encourages liberated thinking? Is your culture supportive of risk-taking and small experiments, or is it one that is risk-averse?

According to the Malcolm Baldrige National Quality Award criteria, *"Innovation means making meaningful change to improve an organization's products, services, programs, processes, operations, and business model to create new value for the organization's stakeholders. Innovation should lead your organization to new dimensions of performance. Innovation is no longer strictly the purview of research and development departments; innovation is important for all aspects of your operations and all work systems and work processes. Organizations should be led and managed so that innovation becomes part of the learning culture. Innovation should be integrated into daily work and should be supported by your performance improvement system."*

Systematic processes for innovation should reach across your entire organization because innovation builds on the accumulated knowledge of your enterprise and its people. Therefore, the ability to rapidly disseminate and capitalize on this knowledge is critical to driving organizational innovation.

There are many questions to explore when looking to build a climate that liberates thinking for innovation.

BUILDING THE CLIMATE TO LIBERATE THINKING: BIAS FOR INNOVATION

• Who in the organization should set the expectation for innovation? innovation?	• How do you sift through all of the information gathered by sensors to find the best opportunities to innovate?
• How do you move new products forward or implement new processes in a company where the old way is working great?	• How can management best communicate what an innovation process is to the larger organization?
• How do you make innovation happen not just in products or processes but also on an organizational level?	• How do you reconcile the human and technological or scientific side of innovation?
• How do you know when to support an innovative idea against internal opponents and when to let the innovation change and evolve?	• How do you create a sustainable innovative culture in an organization?

In 2012, the first four of the fifty most innovative companies listed by *Fast Company* were all technology enterprises—Apple, Facebook, Google, and Amazon. These companies have created transformative industry disruption and opened channels for new opportunities to countless others through fostering the creation of a half-million apps; connecting and enabling social-media networking and rapid communication systems; bringing information and knowledge to billions of people irrespective of race, gender, class or nationality; and providing access and avenues for products and services without limitation of travel or bricks and mortar.

When you liberate thinking, you're creating possibilities and putting high-octane into the fuel for adapting and finding new solutions as the dynamics of change and opportunity converge. It starts by the leadership cadre setting the expectation and creating the positive climate for the bias for innovation.

➤ FOCUSING ON CUSTOMERS

Focusing on customers is a process for ensuring the organization has a detailed understanding of the customers it serves, what their needs are, and how their needs can be better met. One of the key characteristics projected in IBM's Enterprise of the Future study is the idea that successful organizations of the future must develop the capacity to create "innovation beyond your customer's imagination." That outcome only happens through a very high degree of customer focus fueling the innovation cycle. Many organizations believe they understand their customers simply because they have been doing business together for a long time. Unfortunately that attitude can also create blinders, blocking the view of how customers are changing and adapting to their environment and choices. Most good marketers have developed effective mechanisms for getting customer involvement through focus groups, surveys, and interactive creative discovery groups.

Over the years, we have been involved in several very productive creative-discovery projects bringing together heavy-user consumers who offer useful personal insights into the how, why, and what they buy in categories as diverse as banking, personal organizers, outdoor footwear, and even slippers.

There is much to be learned from a thoughtful immersion into the world of your customers or users that can provide you with a ground-floor understanding of what embodies an added value proposition and what is merely a product or service.

The extra magic also happens when organizations bring that same standard of innovation beyond imagination inside the organization in satisfying the needs of internal customers. Customer focus is a critical element of a value system, and organizations will get higher levels of authentic customer care and focus from their team members when they feel the internal culture is characterized by that same care paradigm. In our work conducting organizational audits using The Agile Model, we often see examples of organizations with weak external customer orientation likewise lacking the internal customer orientation. It is extremely difficult for organizations lacking this connectivity and energy to excel in creating ongoing innovation.

Naturally, technology is playing a major role these days in helping to create greater customer focus through the variety of have-it-my-way customizations, for instance MyProfile, MyCart, MyMusic, MyFood, "MyEverything." There is so much customization and personalized service that routinely happens for consumers today that when they are faced with a traditional service lacking that personalization, it just doesn't feel right and they are likely to turn to a competitor who provides customized service.

➤ ENCOURAGING IDEA DIVERSITY

Encouraging idea diversity is a process for making sure new ideas are constantly raised and come from multiple sources both inside and outside the organization. You'll continually get access to better idea generation if all stakeholders in your organization know and feel invited to share their ideas, suggestions, and invention for the good of the company. Idea diversity helps bring freshness to idea generation.

In working through the Agility Core Belief System with clients, we make it clear that organizations must view their people as their first priority if the organization aims to become truly agile. It is when your people feel trusted, respected, valued, and encouraged to share their ideas that you gain access to that 40 percent discretionary-effort bonus.

From what we have seen and experienced in our work, the key to encouraging real idea diversity is in actively setting the table to make idea sharing easier and more frequent. This can become an active part of your strategic process so that mission-critical issues get campaigned for idea generation across the enterprise, encouraging alignment, energy, and connection. Real idea diversity seeks original ideas from all stakeholders rather than just their opinions on your ideas or those generated by the idea department. As with most everything else, driving innovation and people's involvement requires persistent follow-through and leadership creativity.

Driving idea diversity is at the heart of the powerful value proposition in the rapidly growing collaboration software industry discussed earlier where companies such as Citrix and Cisco Systems and others are bringing the capacity for idea sharing and distribution across mega organizations in highly efficient and effective ways that drive innovation traction better and faster.

On the other hand, there are also simpler ways to promote and achieve idea diversity in your organization. One very simple technique we often promote in workshops is using butcher paper or flip chart paper tacked to high traffic hallways where you write a problem statement that invites ideas for how to improve or solve an issue. Team members are provided markers or Post-It notes to visibly share their ideas for all to see and stimulate further ideas. By providing convenient vehicles for engaging your teams and capturing their ideas, you can help shape their path towards idea diversity. You can, as Chip Heath and Dan Heath say in their 2010 book, *Switch*, help them "change when change is hard."

Our experience shows that idea diversity emerges and thrives in a climate that is encouraging and positive. To that end, there are many organizational skills and group dynamics that can be developed and shaped to help promote full involvement from your people. One such simple technique is to build out the power of parallel thinking when bringing your people together for idea generation. Edward deBono is the father of parallel thinking and has compiled a simple but very effective system for people to communicate and collaborate together called Six Thinking Hats. The system works because it provides an easily understood tool that helps teams progressively work through an idea generation or problem-solving exercise by all wearing one hat at a time, thus the name *parallel thinking*.

Future success will increasingly require the capacity to find new solutions—better and faster, and if your organization is not equipped to deliver on this value, your customers will look to your competitors.

➤ TIPS TO HELP YOU LIBERATE THINKING

1. Nothing promotes action more than a contest. You can promote and kick off efforts for more idea generation—and thereby communicate that you want and expect idea generation—by having team or department contests for idea generation. Maybe the first round is a contest on how to generate more ideas?

2. Create an internal customer day promoting communication and sharing feedback on how you can improve mutual service expectations. Each team creates a list of three commitments for change or improvement, including a highly visible measurement system.

3. Initiate a simple monthly gathering for keeping team members engaged and included in what's happening with the organization's journey for success. Always include feedback on idea generation, emphasizing the percentage of team members who contributed to idea generation. You might start with a simple skit, acting out what it looks like to create an idea.

CHAPTER 9

E is for Evaluating Results

There is truth in the old business proverb that what gets measured gets done. Yet one of the many challenges business leaders face in today's fast-paced, change-driven world is determining the "what and how" of measuring relevant organizational performance. Traditional outcome metrics—sales, profits, costs, employee retention, and even customer satisfaction—are important, if not essential. But if they are the only performance measures in your scorecard, you may be navigating your enterprise by looking out the rear window instead of looking forward.

The pace of change, rampant innovation, and rising customer expectation at all levels demand a different and more fluid approach to performance measurement. Getting desired results is the goal of all organizations, and the classic way of determining if results are achieved is evaluation. Many think of evaluation primarily in terms of measurement. It is also a way of determining what was done wrong, if results aren't achieved, and what could have been done differently. Technology has enabled more dynamic, interactive, and real-time capabilities that support nimble and adaptive organizations. Evaluating results demands a clear, aligned, and energetic approach: creating expectations, providing real-time feedback, and ensuring the use of fact-based measures.

➤ CREATING EXPECTATIONS

Creating expectations is a process for making sure that all stakeholders understand your organization's goals, strategies for attaining those goals, and resources that are available for achieving expected outcomes.

It can be said that satisfaction, and maybe even happiness, might be the differential between expectations and reality in what it was you are expecting and what actually happens. Take, for example, when you go out to see a movie that one of your best friends has declared is the best movie she has ever seen and she knows you will just love it. Now, depending on previous experiences when this person may have recommended a restaurant, some music, or maybe a TV show, you may either discount her recommendation or acknowledge that if she liked it, then you would probably like it too. Your previous experiences have validated (or not) similar tastes in similar things.

You arrive at the movie and begin watching expectantly, waiting for it to become one of the best movies you have ever seen. And you wait, and wait, watch, and watch some more; eventually, as the movie ends, you conclude that the movie was just okay, maybe even pretty good. But it certainly did not reach the top tier of movies you had ever seen. Why not? What happened here? You raised the bar on expectations to a level so high that it would be tough for any movie to satisfy, so you came away somewhat disappointed. Had you gone into the same movie with little to no preconceived expectation, you may have come away agreeing you're your friend, claiming the same movie is one of the best movies you had ever seen.

No matter whether you're the owner or boss, a key customer, employee, supplier, someone's sweetheart, or a regular person heading to see a movie, your satisfaction with an outcome or experience relates directly to what you were expecting (or hoping) to happen. In fact, Watson Wyatt (now Towers Watson) conducted several studies on employee engagement over the past several years that have consistently reported two of the top three factors driving individual employee engagement as: (1) the extent to which employees know what is expected from them, and (2) the awareness level for how they are doing vs. expectations from the perspective of their bosses.

This equation involving setting and communicating expectations gets to the heart of the performance management effectiveness crucible and captures the essence of what makes evaluating results a key driver for agility in organizations and individuals. Without recognizing this element of effectively creating expectations as a critical step worth doing well and continuously updating expectations as circumstances change, organizations and leaders will find it very hard to build an execution culture or leadership culture based on true empowerment and accountability. Fuzziness in expectations clouds and inhibits building an execution and accountability culture—the foundation for an agile organization.

Jim Collins introduced the notion that some of the great companies moved from *Good to Great* and stayed so by creating BHAGs (Big Hairy Audacious Goals). Agile organizations are able to set and achieve audacious goals by deploying aligned capability in the five agility drivers. What kind of goals are you creating? Mediocre ones or audacious ones? Hank Steinbrecher is a good friend and former general secretary of the United States Soccer Federation (USSF), the overall governing body for youth, adult, and professional soccer in America. Hank tells a great story of the USSF planning and conducting the 1999 FIFA Women's World Cup hosted by the United States. The dramatic final game had over ninety thousand spectators at the Rose Bowl in Pasadena, California, where Brandi Chastain sealed the victory with her spectacular penalty kick and dramatic sports bra unveiling. Filling the Rose Bowl with ninety-thousand-plus spectators was one of the actual audacious goals set by the organizing team before the start of the competition. Filling the Rose Bowl with fans to watch a women's soccer game in 1999: now that was an audacious goal for certain.

Audacious goals can frustrate and demoralize organizations when the commitment, resources, and steadfast leadership focus do not support the goals. Conversely, they can become incredibly motivating, inspiring organizations, teams, and leaders to accomplish and deliver great things. The difference rests in alignment of expectations, focus, commitment, and resources. As Steinbrecher described the 1999 World Cup adventure, once the USSF set that audacious goal, they then started building audacious fill-the-Rose-Bowl kinds of ideas. Had they established the goal to put forty thousand spectators in the final venue, which would have no doubt been a valid goal, they would have pursued much lower octane spectator initiatives.

➤ PROVIDING REAL-TIME FEEDBACK

Providing real-time feedback is a process for making sure stakeholders give and receive ongoing information about how well they are accomplishing their part of the organization's mission, plus suggestions for how they can improve.

Agile organizations are dynamic and organic. They recognize the speed of transformation and the need to sense and respond quickly as factors in their environment and success model begin to shift dynamically. If you have built an effective sensing and monitoring system for your enterprise, especially one that actively tracks important forces of change, then you will be channeling relevant feedback into your monitoring processes. One of the keys to ratcheting your agility will be the timely streaming of much of that mission-critical feedback as possible to the proper recipients. Dr. Gary Hamel, management expert and founder of Strategos, points to the World Wide Web as one of the great models for organizations building fitness for the future. The web operates open-source in real-time all the time, and thereby has the potential for continuous transformation and growth—virally and organically with transparent, timely feedback at all levels driving real accountability.

Real-time feedback systems are infiltrating many different aspects of everyday life. Gadgets or apps can be purchased with an endless array of applications designed to provide instant action or feedback. Golfers can even buy an attachment to put on their golf clubs that will analyze every swing and provide a full report anytime a player wishes to review it. Another example is the various apps linked to GPS capabilities that allow people to point their phones at restaurants or other retail establishments and get the latest reviews before trying them out. Whether it is Angie's List or simply reviewing the number of stars rated on devices or movies, society is benefiting from the real-time feedback that exists in today's agile world.

Agile organizations need the same kind of rapid bio-feedback information that supports improving personal health. Some of the most meaningful and instructive feedback will come from employees, customers, suppliers, and the field of bio-feedback has many examples of how an organization can adapt progressively as it gets the right insight or information. The latest craze of fitness measurement devices like Fitbit are a good example of streaming together several agile elements besides just real-time feedback. Consider the goal-setting feature in these devices as a means of creating expectations. Most such devices offer opportunity to connect, engage and collaborate with a user-defined community all the while as the device senses and monitors on fact-based measures (steps, heart rate, sleep pattern, etc.).

Technology continues to explode with new possibilities of adaptive solutions with built-in real-time feedback systems that enable automatic synchronous adjustments. It's the human system that has more challenges in giving and digesting real-time feedback, and then making the corresponding behavior adjustments.

➤ INSURING THE USE OF FACT-BASED MEASURES

Conducting fact-based measurement is a process for insuring that judgments about whether outcome and performance expectations are met are grounded in reliable, valid, and relevant information linked to your definition of success. Here are some of the considerations for building your fact-based measurement system.

- How can you create individual dashboards that reflect customer-based outcome measures for both internal and external customers?

- What facts are most relevant to the customers and how can we go about collecting the facts, tracking in real-time without creating huge new bureaucracy?

- How do you define the right Key Agility Indicators (KAIs) for each area of the enterprise so those areas can become more proactive and accountable not dependent on management reviews to initiate and implement corrective actions?

These considerations also impact the effectiveness of your collaboration by how well you build expectations and rigor into your decision process and team project management systems.

Consider a dashboard approach. Just as modern-day cars are programmed with various warning lights to pinpoint excess variability or signal potential trouble spots, business analytic dashboards are designed to give the executive or any user a series of dials, gauges, and warning lights that enable rapid detection of trouble spots by following simple green, yellow, and red light signals. The premise is to leverage the power of technology so that executive attention can be rapidly channeled to the pressure and leverage points (variances in revenues, costs, quality, customer service, and so on) where value-added leadership attention is needed. The notion of computer-aided dashboards for tracking and guiding performance has become very well developed over the past several years. The latest examples of business analytic dashboards from providers such as SAS Institute are increasingly sophisticated and robust in their capability to synthesize data into actionable insight at incredible speed.

Clearly, technology exists that enables the timely monitoring of organizational activity in real-time but a question remains: What should you be measuring? Your measurement choices actually define your real de-facto priorities and create focus for the organization.

The concept of a balanced scorecard was developed by Harvard professors Robert Kaplan and David Norton way back in the early 1990s and is still evolving. The balanced scorecard concept promotes the inclusion of four primary perspectives into your measurement system: the traditional financial view, measures of core business processes, the voice of the customer, and measures of the organization's ability to learn and grow. These domains represent important forces in the organizational success equation. The key is to find ways to define specific measures for each area that can be reliably measured in real-time and that align with the core value proposition (CVP) for the organization. Making sure that your measurement is always linked to the CVP is the grounding that makes these metrics meaningful and instructive for your organization. Since Kaplan and Norton brought forward the notion of balanced scorecards, there has been much evolution of understanding and use of these kinds of scorecards, and also new technology drivers that bring much greater rigor and automation to the dashboarding of success measures. The intent of the balanced scorecard concept is to fundamentally reassess and define the most accurate success measures for the enterprise, taking into account more than just the traditional financial metrics. This notion of balance is a key concept used in the construction of strategy maps and determination of the metrics for success codified in that process.

When looking at measuring core business processes, leaders aspiring to help their organizations become more agile will want to include performance metrics on the other four drivers of organizational agility as well—for instance, how well the organization anticipates change, generates confidence with employees and customers, initiates action through speed of decision-making at all levels, and generates volumes of valuable new ideas because leadership has created the environment for liberated thinking.

These drivers represent the Key Agility Indicators (KAI) for the organization or team. Key agility indicators are the vital signs of agile organizations and for leaders who are ready to adapt and thrive in the twenty-first century, achieving new levels of readiness to face unknown levels of turbulence and uncertainty. This level of readiness is not discretionary if you want to survive. How do you translate these drivers for greater nimbleness and adaptability into your organization or your industry? What are the best indicators or measures of being focused, fast, and flexible in your context?

Certainly as you compare your organization's to your key competitors' capabilities or your key customers' expectations, you will be provided with feedback on how focused you are in understanding their needs, trends, and shifting directions. How well can you anticipate change? How about your speed to market with new ideas or speed to find and implement cost improvement projects? What is the flexibility that is needed most in your business to adapt and change, plug and play, or morph when your customer expectations change? Building the dynamic capability within your organizations and within each of your leaders—to sense and respond better and faster—is an imperative for future survival.

Evaluating results is important because these practices help align all stakeholders in the focus of how you define and measure success—for yourselves, your customers, and all other key stakeholders.

➤ TIPS TO HELP YOU EVALUATE RESULTS

1. How clear are the key priorities for each of your people, teams, functions, or units? Are the expectations fresh and current or old and stale from a few years ago? Are they implicit where you hope people understand or explicit and include a personal conversation within the past three months?

2. Do you have a mechanism for timely feedback with your key people, customers, and suppliers, and at least a monthly review of key performance indicators? How about key agility indicators?

3. Does each person, team, unit, and function have a dashboard of success that captures the four to five key vital signs of organizational health and vitality? Are they aligned to your overall strategy map and enterprise dashboard of agility and success?

SECTION THREE:
Creating the Agility Advantage

During 2011 to 2013, Valerus embraced The Agile Model as a framework to help define and drive its transformation in the oil and gas handling and processing sector. Valerus entered a severe downturn in 2008 as the price of natural gas fell to new lows. The senior leadership committed to hire and train leaders with agility to change the company and build sustainable success. Leaders were coached and trained to apply The Agile Model to their day-to-day work. Through the Accelerated Leadership Development Program (ALDP), a talent assessment and management process, the company identified the Valerus high potential leaders who worked on teams to solve key business issues facing the company.

The company HR group aligned The Agile Model with its approach to talent assessment, performance management, leadership development, team development, and employee engagement processes within the company. As an illustration, HR built agility into its talent review process by integrating scenario planning with the process so that it could adjust and adapt its talent portfolio with the demands of a turbulent marketplace. The Valerus business results of 46 percent revenue growth, year over year, for 2011 to 2013, combined with a similar EBITDA growth over the same time period of 21 percent, lends credibility to the business impact of this organizational agility transformation process.

CHAPTER 10

Leveraging Agility Collaboration

Thus far, we have described in detail the accelerating forces that are at work in our hyper-turbulent, or VUCA, world. We have presented the components of The Agile Model, which was created to help leaders understand the range and types of responses that are necessary for organizations, groups, and individuals to respond effectively to these conditions, and also to help leaders identify the practical thinking that has been done by a number of management experts.

Now the question is: What specific steps need to be taken in order to make use of this model in building your own agile organization? In other words, how is agility implemented?

You can follow a series of sequential steps, a roadmap, for the journey of transforming your organization into an agile enterprise. Before starting this journey, it is essential you know where you are with respect to a particularly important aspect of transformation: your values and the Agility Core Belief System introduced in chapter 2.

➤ THE IMPORTANCE OF CORE VALUES

Where you are going and where you are presently underscore the importance of understanding your values. There's an old story about the English businessman who was traveling and got lost deep in the Irish countryside. When he stopped to ask a crusty old Irish farmer for directions to Dublin, the farmer says, "Well, sir, I wouldn't start from here." You must always recognize the reality of where you are—both strategically and culturally—even if it is not where you would like to be.

In the effort to become agile, a true transformative journey will bring you to a place where everyone in the organization shares critical core values. Agile organizations are better equipped to embrace and excel with the agile drivers when the core values outlined in the Agility Core Belief System are present and actively aligned.

1. The future will always be VUCA

2. Agility is a survival imperative

3. People are paramount

4. Focused, fast and flexible shared mindset essential

5. Agile culture fuels success

6. Agile operating principles matter

These core belief tenets operate as a code of conduct or as guidelines for working together in an agile organization. If there is significant deviation from the leadership behavior called for in this value system, it results in additional drag that slows and confuses the organization. While the journey will never really be over, where your values are as you start the process will have a significant impact on the length and pain of your journey. The further your values are from the values of a high-functioning agile organization, the greater the amount of fundamental change management will be involved in your transformation. If you are too far away, it will be hard to get to agility from there. The closer your organization is to this set of core beliefs and values, the more likely you will be able to succeed in establishing and sustaining agility.

In beginning your agility effort, it is important to recognize that transformation is not easy. It may take your organization two to three years or longer to achieve basic framework to support agility, depending upon how much pain you are willing to endure and how close your existing value system or culture already are to the tenets outlined in the Agility Core Belief System. That said, the alternative—having your organization torn apart by ever-increasing turbulence—should be a powerful motivator.

➤ A ROADMAP FOR AGILITY

Because it will take time, commitment, and careful attention, building agility is best approached as a journey. We have developed a roadmap to guide you through the progression addressing the issues and actions that will reward you with the transformation you seek. This roadmap will take you through five steps: mobilize, envision, plan, deploy, and sustain. These steps are sequential but overlap to some degree. Throughout the journey you will use The Agile Model to track where you are and to help move you forward.

ROADMAP FOR CREATING AGILITY ADVANTAGE ... BECOMING FOCUSED, FAST & FLEXIBLE

MOBILIZE	ENVISION	PLAN	DEPLOY	SUSTAIN
Establish the Agility Imperative	Shape the Agility Advantage	Build the Integration Priorities	Ignite, Educate and Involve	Engrain, Grow and Leverage

CHAPTER 11

Mobilizing for Agility

As mentioned previously, any effort at organizational change and transformation is hard. This *is* the reality. Becoming an agile organization requires significant commitment, determination, and at times even true courage. As you begin this journey, you must take what we call *the mobilize step*. The purpose of this step is to prepare your organization for the journey—especially important in getting all of senior leadership on board. This will require you to: first, make sure everyone in the organization understands the need for individuals, teams, and the organization as a whole to be agile in this VUCA world—in other words, to define and accept the agile imperative in your own team; second, to set the parameters of the agility effort, taking care that everyone knows and buys into them; and, third, to create the core team that will spearhead the work.

Establishing the compelling need for your organization to become more agile is essential, prefaced by the leadership team being asked the critical question of "Why must we change?" The burning platform for why we have to change and why agility is essential must be posed, examined, prosecuted, and concluded with a positive verdict—a firm and geniune decision. There have been numerous cases of senior leadership lip service and ambiguity that resulted in diminished results or protracted delays in the progress of organizational transformation. Everyone on your senior leadership team (including directors and owners) must see the same need and feel the same sense of urgency.

Even with a strong belief in change, and senior leadership committed to change, you can and will encounter some formidable negative inertia. Organizations vary greatly in terms of the determining factors causing inertia. What is at the center of your operational universe? Is your organization highly customer-driven? Are your operations highly centered by the dynamics of product innovation? Is your organization lauded for your unique manufacturing or logistics capabilities? What will keep agility moving forward within your organization is the strong linkage between core strategy and the creation of competitive advantage. Organizations and teams must continually ask and answer these questions: Why must we be more agile? Why must we build superior capacity to sense and respond better and faster? How will agility help us be more successful and create more value in our organization?

The essence of mobilization is to discover the intrinsic linkage to the why, how, and what statements of organizational purpose, process, and measurement. This keeps the drive behind agility fresh, relevant and replenished.

In making sure your leaders understand and are committed to the drive to be agile, it is important they understand what the scope of the agility effort will be. A clear mission statement will address this need and also help everyone maintain their bearings throughout the journey.

Just as teams are the juggernaut of overall organizational success, teams play a key role in the success of the transformation to an agile organization. There will be an implementation team driving the effort, as well as numerous teams concerned with various components, so the team development process is a significant part of the mobilization step.

Initial efforts to begin a systematic approach to analyzing, assessing, and building an agility development plan will require a project team approach, usually utilizing a mix of internal and external resources. The nature of the mix is a function of each organization's philosophy towards resources. Some organizations maintain very limited staff-support services and tend to utilize external expertise in a just-in-time dosage for special services as needed. Other organizations have a heavy bias towards internal line resources being accountable for solving and implementing changes needed, believing that if real change is to be sustained, it must be owned and driven by company line managers. Both approaches can be successful, and there are definitely benefits and drawbacks with each.

	ACTION STEPS	CRITICAL QUESTIONS
MOBILIZE	• Establishing and acknowledging compelling need and drive for becoming more agile • Develops the agility implementation scope and mission statement and initiates team development process	1. What is the compelling need and burning platform for agility in your organization? 2. Does everyone on your ownership and senior leadership team see the same need and feel the same sense of urgency and buy into the Agile Core Belief System? 3. Have you identified the right mix of internal and external resources capable of guiding and championing the efforts?

CHAPTER 12

Envisioning Agility

I t is often said, "If you don't know where you're going, any road will take you there." That certainly applies to the agility development journey. The most successful transformations we have witnessed and facilitated are those that have identified clear sequential destinations along this long-term journey to develop true agility.

The envision step's purpose is to gain a clear idea of the organization's current situation (where it is) and to project its desired ideal state (where it wants to go). This phase begins with a focus on assessing and defining what will be your organization's key business components. You might assess such issues as the agility of your corporate processes, the level of commitment of key champions and sponsors, the effectiveness of communication channels and existing communication protocols, and training needs. You will define such components as strategic objectives, stakeholders, values, and competitive edge. In considering the journey from your current situation to your desired state, you will also lay out the business case, purpose, and nature of the transformation to agility.

The Agile Model provides an excellent framework for making a systematic assessment of focus, speed, adaptability, and leadership behavior that builds perspective on competitive effectiveness. We call this type of systematic organizational assessment using The Agile Model an Agility Audit with a diagnostic report called the Organizational Agility Profile (OAP).

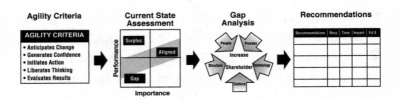

The Organizational Agility Profile (OAP) is a rigorous and detailed assessment process providing a comprehensive examination of the seventy-five touchpoints for organizational agility tied to the five drivers in The Agile Model. The agility audit also includes a set of qualitative questions and stakeholder interviews to explore the organization context and forces of change necessary to develop an agility gap analysis to confirm obstacles and agility development priorities.

There are many classic organizational assessment tools that can be applied as a framework for examining your current condition. The key is in which questions you consider as you examine the dimensions of your organization. For example, "How does our structure help or hurt us to anticipate change or generate confidence?"

may be a question that needs to be asked. One of the most rigorous and respected frameworks for examining organizational effectiveness is the Malcolm Baldrige National Quality Award process. The extensive movement towards total quality dates back into the late 1970s and early 1980s. The Baldrige framework of critical organizational processes provides an additional level of rigor to prosecute the key agility question of how an organization will become more focused, fast, and flexible in this VUCA world.

The defining aspect of this step can help with a number of issues. The organization's strategic framework will create renewable energy and focus for your organization and the agility journey. The basic elements of an agile strategy map are in chapter 5 within the discussion of visioning, but the elements bear repeating. Each of these elements can drive focus and enthusiasm across your team.

The development of your agile strategy map can generate important clarity for the transformation journey and also can provide a strategic cleansing. This is not to say that strategy maps are a new invention. Certainly the power of focused, concise, and value-based strategies that cascade throughout organizations of every denomination has been championed and reported throughout recorded time. But a strategy map is an essential aspect of any agility effort in that it clearly defines what we must be agile about.

This engage step is also where you should set forth your expectations for the speed of capability-building in addressing your agility gaps, as well as the outcomes that should emerge from thoughtful examination of your current situation. Defining how fast you intend to go in addressing the gaps and building new capability is a most important step because it will often also define how much "pain of change" you should expect. Just as going too slow is problematic, going too fast can be just as problematic.

Understanding your desired outcomes is important—at the enterprise level and at every level in the organization. It is what continuously reinforces the notion of why agility matters and why investing time, energy, and resources in its pursuit must be a priority. The stronger the clarity and importance of the definitions of where you want to be, the stronger the commitment and personal energy that will be invested at all levels.

Images of leaders building their fitness and nimbleness to walk across dangerous ravines on tightropes carrying long poles to provide balance come to mind. How do you get to your goals across the ravines with all kinds of turbulence swirling around you? The vision/value proposition on one side and the values/culture on the other side of the pole provide the balance agile leaders need to reach their goals. This is a skill to be built at all levels.

	ACTION STEPS	CRITICAL QUESTIONS
ENVISION	• Analyzes the current situation and defines the business case, purpose, and nature of the transformation to agility. • Articulating vision of strategic objectives, stakeholders, values, and edge by building the strategy map.	1. What are the conclusions and implications from the agility audit with regard to the agile capabilities of your people, processes, and technology? 2. After framing your strategic intent into a strategy map summary, what are the strategic priorities and improvement needs for your focus, speed, and flexibility? 3. What are the goals and outcomes you expect from building greater organizational agility? By when?

CHAPTER 13

Planning for Agility

The purpose of *the plan step* is to determine specifically how to get from where you are to where you want to be. To do this, you must develop a strategic agility plan to identify the key agility indicators for the overall business, define critical roles in the implementation process for internal and external resources, determine which mission-critical initiatives will require corporate project team initiation, develop educational curriculum and content, determine the number of internal and external facilitator resources needed, and build a communications plan for rollout of education and development programming.

In the plan step, you must pay particular attention to the issue of mission-critical gaps and to the necessity of carrying out education and development to systematically build organizational skills in those areas.

Building a company-wide agility education process helps create and deliver great clarity around the strategic importance of agility along with the shared beliefs, operating principles, and specific tools to aid in the journey. The educational process, when implemented, will be very beneficial in helping to root the journey to agility and build enthusiasm in addition to capability. Experience shows agility education across the company helps generate confidence as team members build enhanced collaboration, decision-making and problem-solving skills, which also boost job success, productivity, and personal enrichment. Additional development activity such as leadership coaching and action team projects will help align focus on critical agility gaps because the learning experience is supported with action application in the learning process, thus developing better understanding through building skill with the right tools and key agility concepts.

A critical part of the plan process is your agility audit in which the five drivers of The Agile Model are analyzed with respect to people, process, and technology. Using the audit, most organizations are able to identify three to five mission-critical gaps that make agility difficult to achieve. Sometimes these gaps appear to be just the usual organizational weaknesses, for instance, the need to improve communication or increase employee involvement. More often, what emerges is a fresh realization of the impact of internal ambiguity around priorities and values, along with a multitude of mixed signals, largely inadvertent, that end up paralyzing one or more critical enterprise processes. The senior leadership team has a great opportunity to make an important statement about their commitment to the journey by incorporating the learning and outcomes from the audit into the plan for education and development activities. This is especially powerful when they make clear and visible changes to their own behavior as a result of insights gained in the process.

Building a cascading education plan that helps people see the need for agility is one of the most important steps in this journey. Some organizations have a pattern of introducing new transformation every other year and approach this step as if they were planning the fashion color scheme for this year's corporate window dressing. Needless to say, those organizations hardly ever get traction on anything significant because everyone knows that this too shall pass.

Every education process is unique because each organization has its own history, organizational dynamics, and competitive framework. Successful education is aligned and delivered in a strategic context that not only frames the agile pathway for enterprise success, but also embraces and illuminates the pathway for team member success. Planning and deploying the right combination of education and information in this step can create the equivalent of an organic cleansing, where an organization can purge earlier or conflicting versions of how it creates success and its mission-critical priorities. This is an important opportunity to communicate both the Agility Core Belief System and the unique set of core values and expectations for the organization.

The best approach to communicating and educating client teams in the concepts, applications, and tools associated with The Agile Model is in building highly interactive workshop experiences that provide a blended and discovery-style learning approach. These learning modules need to be tailored to both the learning and application levels of the participants if you expect to get maximum understanding and traction. Each of the five drivers in The Agile Model have both conceptual and practical dimensions that should be linked to help team members understand and apply them for full impact and traction. One of The Agile Model's strengths is that the number of tools that can be used to build out capability in any of the fifteen primary agility processes is unlimited.

A good example is in the area of building better and faster capability for decision-making and problem-solving. As discussed in chapter 7, we promote the use of Boyd's OODA LOOP method in our practice. This is by no means the only structured decision-making or problem-solving method that could be used, and if your organization favors the plan-do-check-act approach or the DMAIC model used in Six-Sigma environments, that's fine. Tailoring your toolkit to fit your culture will help in building acceptance as long as you are getting the outcomes you strive for in building capability. Continuous improvement has no boundaries.

The education phase also represents a great opportunity to integrate learning and organizational development activity at the same time. This will raise the bar on understanding and engagement as you use this as an occasion to educate your team on the mission-critical gap areas and invite their ideas and energy through the learning process (as a beginning). This effort helps senior leaders establish a key basis for achieving agility through creating focus. Your education and learning design should include a focus on your critical gaps so that many of the exercises used to help the teams understand how to learn and apply the agile drivers also provide deeper connectivity and understanding about these critical improvement areas. This engagement process is also an opportunity to launch ongoing localized efforts to keep the focus on improvement activity in the strategically important areas that will bring aligned business impact in each location and function.

ACTION STEPS	CRITICAL QUESTIONS
• Conduct the agility analytics and audit to determine your gaps and priorities for how to move from your current to desired state of agility. • Articulate and define the entire process required to establish framework for agility aligned across people, process, and technology.	1. What are the mission-critical gaps and priorities for your agility improvement process? 2. How can your plan for deployment demonstrate the commitment of senior leaders and influencers? 3. How do you implement highly visible key metrics for improving the mission-critical gaps and plan for each unit to define its own mission-critical gaps and priorities?

PLAN

CHAPTER 14

Deploying Agility

The *deploy step* is where your actual implementation begins and real traction starts. There is a critical difference between programs that are deployed as new training initiatives versus the introduction of new success models or operating principles linked to creating sustainable success for all stakeholders. Too many times employees see the new program of the year introduced with slogans and fanfare. Then they just go through the motions, knowing that if they keep heads low and nodding, they'll make it through another seasonal fad.

We believe the deployment of agility-building activities will be substantially more effective and aligned if designed and delivered in the form of a strategy and engagement deployment. This deployment step is where your organization's business model for success and its core operating values are introduced or reaffirmed and put into action as you begin to deploy education and development time and energy across the organization.

In the deploy step, you will build understanding and commitment to agility principles, engage staff towards the new goals or outcomes, and establish new ways of working as individuals and in teams. You'll also introduce the strategic focusing system for cascading strategy maps as well as establish and implement key agility indicators and dashboards for measuring and tracking traction and success. This step builds high-impact focus and understanding of the key issues that drive value and customer satisfaction. Using action-learning and involvement approaches such as discovery maps or customized simulations help teams at all levels experience the transformation first-hand through high-engagement discovery-learning methods versus traditional talk-at-you management meetings.

Another critical ingredient in successful deployment involves the active involvement of you and your senior leadership. You are not deploying a program for everyone else. You are deploying a new system for how the organization and its leadership can build progressive capability to face and adapt together as the context for your success continues to evolve. Deploy works best when top leaders create relevant expectations and actually use the outputs from the process. It becomes hollow when teams go through the expected motions and the real focus and work turn out to be completely separate and unconnected.

ACTION STEPS	CRITICAL QUESTIONS
• Build understanding and commitment to agility principles, introduces staff towards the new goals or outcomes, and establishes new ways of working as individuals and in teams • Introduce the strategic focusing system for cascading strategy maps • Establish and implement key agility indicators and dashboards for measuring and tracking traction and success	1. What is the extent of behavior change or learning new behaviors involved in your deployment? 2. How will you align and connect your strategic focusing process as an integral aspect of agility development and to keep agility efforts focused on mission-critical areas of need and return? 3. How will you build a dashboard to assess and track success in deployment of the agile development process?

DEPLOY

CHAPTER 15

Sustaining Agility

There's no question that the most distinctive part of this transformation is sustaining agility once you have put the framework in place. You can't just arrive at your desired state and then forget about keeping with it. In fact, your journey will be continual because the VUCA forces will continue to impact you and every aspect of your organization. You must keep moving and looping back through the other roadmap steps in order to maintain your desired state.

The sustain step represents an ongoing effort with the purpose of maintaining and refreshing relevancy of the first four steps. Depending on corporate history, it can be relatively easy or decidedly difficult to marshal the energy for an ongoing corporate-wide initiative to sustain agility, which might be seen as a series of additional initiatives. For some organizations, it may seem easy. The extent of a transformational challenge is directly related to the amount of change involved, and maintaining may require fewer changes than the initial effort. For others, it may be the toughest part of the transformation effort. Just as a three-pack-a-day smoker would tell you that it is not the quitting part that is hard, but the not-starting-again part; some organizations will have trouble not relapsing back into fixed, fragile habits. But easy or hard, you don't want the organization to slip back into the reactive malaise of unresponsiveness.

You will begin discovering some of the benefits from building capability with the agile drivers starting to bloom by the time you are in the sustain mode, refreshing the energy and drive of agility in your enterprise. The full thrust of sustain is about how to build ongoing capability for the outcomes of The Agile Model—organizational focus, speed at recognizing issues and seizing opportunities, and the flexibility to avoid or minimize trouble as the market or environmental context shifts.

Some of the actions that must be taken in order to sustain your agility organization are:

- Supporting the cultural change to empowerment of the workforce

- Keeping strategy map priorities and agility initiatives aligned

- Building in measurement processes to assess progress of agility implementation and the learning that has occurred

- Conducting quarterly strategic review and assessment to keep traction on the mission-critical initiatives

- Maintaining aligned talent-management and leadership-development processes

- Reviewing and aligning incentive, recognition, and rewards processes

- Keeping the customer focus of innovation efforts at all levels

	ACTION STEPS	CRITICAL QUESTIONS
SUSTAIN	• Support cultural change and empowerment of the workforce and builds in measurement processes to assess progress of agility implementation and the learning that has occurred. • Involve on-going quarterly strategic review and assessment to get traction on the mission-critical initiatives • On-going talent management and leadership development using the Leadership Agility Profile 360 and Resource Guide.	1. How have you been able to link the focus on agility development with performance feedback and rewards systems within your company? 2. Does your talent review and promotion practice consider leadership agility competency areas? 3. Are you able to establish annual or bi-annual agility audit benchmarking to monitor and track progress and on-going areas needing attention?

THE NEVER-ENDING JOURNEY:

The Future of Agility

Most leaders today are striving to make their organizations more nimble and adaptable. During the past ten years, however, perhaps as many as 80 percent of organizations have tried to implement some form of change initiative to increase speed, flexibility or agility. Based on research studies by Project Management Institute and others, few of those efforts have succeeded. Most of the time the failure can be attributed to internal factors such as slow and convoluted decision making and ambiguous decision rights, siloed barriers between functions, and lack of shared commitment to organizational goals.

Harvard Business School Professor Dr. John Kotter's model for leading change can show why leaders fail to implement agility. According to this view, change efforts typically fail because of the following problems:

- Lack of true senior management commitment or sense of urgency uniformly applied across the whole team.

- Failure to systematically remove obstacles to positive change, whether manifested in outdated processes or technology or people unwilling or unable to adapt.

- Inadequate communication of the positive way forward to build and confirm change down through the organization.

- Failure to recognize and celebrate short-term wins that energize the change, which results in the change effort running out of gas.

- Failure to truly recognize the depth of culture change necessary to anchor new standards. Transformational efforts must go far beyond the lip service of the moment and require occasional tough decisions to demonstrate the integrity of the new operating system.

Efforts to transform organizations into agile enterprises fall prey to the same problems.

These frame many of the reasons for failure. We hope that if you see the world through a lens similar to what we have described here that you will consider and attempt to apply some of the tools and suggestions we have outlined. The journey ahead will no doubt be daunting and filled with challenges and opportunities.

Hyper-turbulence is a phenomenon that has been around for a long time. In 1970, Alvin Toffler peered deep into the soul of what he saw as the future and recognized the basic issue now plainly seen when he pointed out that society was undergoing enormous structural change and that the accelerated rate of technological and social change could overwhelm people.

What would Toffler think if he were to make a return visit now? Would our twenty-first century society reflect the rate of accelerated technological and social change he anticipated? What if he had been in Tunisia or Egypt during the Arab spring? Or would he have a seizure and then ponder the natural next question: What lies ahead during the next forty years?

No doubt we live in an era of accelerated technological and social change. It is the new VUCA normal described in detail throughout this book. The key issue is whether the viscosity of chaotic change will continue to overwhelm people and organizations, causing that increased sense of disconnectedness, stress, and disorientation?

➤ SURVIVAL OF THE FITTEST IN A HYPERTURBULENT WORLD

The idea that the fittest have survived since the beginning of time was famously chronicled in the 1860s when economic philosopher Herbert Spencer coined the phrase after reading Charles Darwin's work *On the Origin of Species*. Will this concept apply to organizations during the next decade in the Age of Agility, with most surviving organizations having built a baseline of speed and adaptability in their business models? How will organizations differentiate themselves in the next generation? Can you afford to wait and see?

While the lens providing details of the future is cloudy in many respects, the VUCA of the future will not only continue to accelerate and intensify, so will its consequences. Yale Professor Foster's projection almost takes your breath away, imagining the disappearance or transformation of hundreds of companies and thousands of jobs.

The agile imperative—the compelling need to develop agility in people, processes, and technology in order to respond to hyperturbulence—will not only continue to be important to organizations in the next few years, but will clearly become the single most important challenge they face.

Given that scenario, we believe that your people will need to be the crucial agility domain going forward. This will play out in several areas: the pursuit of agile talent, reconciling work/home life compression and balance, and enabling more humanity at work. These issues, and more, can be successfully navigated by considering and employing The Agile Model and agile roadmap as a guide for the journey.

➤ GETTING THE PEOPLE PART RIGHT

The people part is superordinate in building an adaptive, agile enterprise. The evidence of the primacy of people will continue to manifest as the intricacy and complexity of globalization and breathtaking change dominate the landscape, making high speed, multi-linear collaboration across the stakeholder network a key competitive differentiator. The following outline shows our perspective on the people equation in this VUCA world through the lens of The Agile Model.

THE AGILE MODEL IMPLICATIONS FOR PEOPLE DEVELOPMENT IN A VUCA WORLD

ANTICIPATING CHANGE	• Strengthening leadership and workforce understanding about the dynamics of change and adaptability • Strengthening understanding of what being more strategic really means in practical terms and how you do that systematically with discipline • Building greater skills for mapping and monitoring forces of change and understanding analytical tools
GENERATING CONFIDENCE	• Enhancing skills for communicating in a real-time world • Active listening embraces generational, technology, and active connectivity with customers • Higher order leadership skills in building trust, commitment, engagement, and enrichment of experience for all stakeholder groups
INITIATING ACTION	• Skills to create focused and aligned sense of urgency • Higher order of decision-making process understanding and skill for leaders and workforce to enable lower and faster levels • Enhanced skills for team and cross-functional collaboration, influencing and conflict resolution techniques to make effective collaboration a competitive advantage
LIBERATING THINKING	• Breaking down traditional paradigms inhibiting creativity; building understanding and skills in parallel thinking and other processes that produce enhanced innovation • Building coaching and facilitation skills in leadership ranks
EVALUATING RESULTS	• Understanding the framework of leadership accountability building in a positive and aligned way • Enhanced skills in defining expectations and making of commitments • Greater skill in performance metrics and timely feedback

Efforts to transform and develop your existing workforce to become more agile are critically important, and finding ways to ensure that new additions to your workforce are built for agility will be essential. We have worked with a research team over several years to explore and map the body of knowledge in the fields of adaptability and human performance as it relates to the notion of selection and development for agility in the workforce. This work has led to some strong conclusions about the opportunity to build a more adaptive and agile workforce through improved selection. Our research indicates there are five dimensions in the agile team member: focus, confidence, proactivity, optimism, and inquisitiveness.

These dimensions and attributes are largely the same ones to work to bring out in existing team members through education and development activities. Certain individuals possess more of these traits than others—whether socialized from birth or shaped over time. Those organizations that can operate with a higher percentage of these qualities in the workforce can find competitive advantage opportunity.

AGILITY PERSONALITY PROFILE

FOCUS	Tends to create goals and concentrate upon them until completion. Stays on track even when it is difficult to do so. Becomes fully engaged in tasks
CONFIDENCE	Approaches work with a sense of self-assuredness. Has a high degree of trust in own abilities. Eager to face challenges
PROACTIVITY	Avoids a reactive mindset. Anticipates tasks and continually looks for ways to make progress. Accepts the need to act without complete information
OPTIMISM	Looks for positive aspects of difficult situations. Bounces back after failing to achieve. Finds hidden opportunities within problems or challenges. Likes team collaboration
INQUISITIVENESS	Values the opportunity to learn. Comfortable in new situations. Seeks and benefits from experiences that demand the acquisition of new knowledge or skill.

A look to the future indicates an increasing importance in attracting and retaining high quality agile talent that possesses the right set of dynamic traits matched with the right kind of skills and experiences to shape your organizational agility advantage.

➤ DESPERATELY SEEKING WORK/HOME LIFE BALANCE

There's another continuing and perplexing issue associated with the increasing pace and VUCA called leadership compression. Leadership compression is that exhausted feeling that many leaders experience daily as they strive to live up to the do-more-and-faster-with-less mantra that prevails in many circles. This is the Toffler *Future Shock* effect of shattering stress and disorientation on steroids. There is only one time zone and everyone's in it—it's the *now* time zone.

Information overload continues to take casualties as the flood of streaming data crushes those who are not able to adapt personal survival practices around enhanced focus, decision-making, time management, and effective use of technology tools. Even with efforts to become advanced in these skills, many are losing the sense of personal competence and confidence. They can't keep up, and that fear saps the potential energy from the idea of work/life balance. The constancy of access via 24/7 communications adds to the complexity.

This dynamic will become an increasing source of conflict and tension as incoming generations may have different value systems around work/home life priorities and the search for meaning and purpose in their lives.

➤ FINDING HUMANITY AT WORK

Successful organizations of the future will genuinely integrate whole life meaning into their mainstream agendas and activities. Genuine generosity is less about just giving financial resources to a charity of choice and more about identifying meaningful, relevant ways for team members to feel connected and make a difference in community and society. The notion of creating genuinely generous corporate ecosystems speaks to the kind of alignment of meaning, purpose, and added value that will resonate now and with the generations to come. This alignment to the broader world and society is becoming increasingly meaningful to both the current, and especially, the emerging generations—the Millennials and generation F—the Facebook generation, as Dr. Gary Hamel declares them to be.

Failure in creating alignment adds one more element of potential drag to organizational speed, questions around alignment of values, and generosity.

Desperately seeking more humanity at work is one more force of change to be considered, and one we believe (and hope) will continue to expand in its relevance and impact. We continue to see evidence of both the importance and leaders striving to build mindfulness of the human spirit and team member well being in global organizations. Sandy Costa is former COO at Quintilles Transnational Corporation who led a meteoric growth spurt of over forty acquisitions and nearly a billion in revenue growth. In 2008, Sandy authored "Humanity at Work" which chronicles some of the challenges and stories to be discovered as we seek to encourage and respect the human spirit in the workplace.

➤ LOOKING FORWARD

We believe the real secret sauce in looking to the future and staying agile lies in your organization's openness and receptivity to new possibilities. The framework of The Agile Model provides a directional instrument for facing the future. Its most critical aspect is found in the continual refreshment of tools, techniques, and methods of stakeholder involvement so you can anticipate change, generate confidence, initiate action, liberate thinking, and always evaluate your results to get better and faster at exceeding those stakeholder dreams—every day. Best wishes for a rewarding and renewing journey.

APPENDIX A:

References

FOCUSED, FAST & FLEXIBLE REFERENCE NOTATIONS

Books

Santo J. Costa, Esq., *Humanity at Work*, 2008

Vince Poscente, *The Age of Speed*, 2008

Alan Axelrod, *Gandhi CEO*, 2010

Gary Hamel, *The Future of Management*, 2007

Dan Heath and Chip Heath, *Switch: How to Change Things When Change Is Hard*, 2010

James L. Heskett, Thomas O. Jones, Gary W. Loveman, W. Earl Sasser, Jr. and Leonard A. Schlesinger; *Service Profit Chain*, 1994

John Fleming and Jim Asplund, *Human Sigma: Managing Employee-Customer Encounter*, 2007

Scott Keller and Colin Price, *Beyond Performance: How Great Organizations Build Create Competitive Advantage*, 2011

Alvin Toffler, *Future Shock*, 1970

Don Sull, *The Upside of Turbulence*, 2009

Rosabeth Moss Kanter, *Confidence*, 2006

Simon Sinek, *Start With Why*, 2009

Simon Sinek, *Leaders Eat Last*, 2013

John Kotter, *Sense of Urgency*, 2008

John Kotter, *Leading Change*, 1996

Stephen M. R. Covey, *The Speed of Trust: The One Thing that Changes Everything*, 2006

Col. John, R., Boyd, *The Essence of Winning and Losing*, 1995

Jim Collins, *Good to Great*, 2005

Jim Collins, *Great By Choice*, 2011

Articles

Philpot, Stacey, "Lessons from Blackberry's Accelerated Obsolescence," *FORBES*, February 25, 2013

Moore, Karl, "Agility: The Ingredient That Will Define Next Generation Leadership," *FORBES*, June 12, 2012

Hamel, Gary, "The Quest for Resilience," *Harvard Business Review*, September 2003

Kaplan, Robert S. and Norton, David P., "Using the Balanced Scorecard as a Strategic Management System," *Harvard Business Review*, July 2007

Other

IBM Global Services, "Global CEO Study," 2010, 2012, 2014

Corporate Executive Board, "Driving Performance and Retention Through Employee Engagement," 2004

Jay Galbraith, "The STAR Model," www.jaygalbraith.com

American Management Association, "The Keys to Strategy Execution," 2007

The Economist Intelligence Unit, "How Businesses Can Survive and Thrive in a Turbulent World," 2009

Malcolm Baldrige Quality Award, http://www.nist.gov/baldrige

Fast Company "2012 Top 50 Most Innovative Companies,"

http://www.fastcompany.com/section/most-innovative-companies-2012

Edward DeBono, "Six Hats Thinking," http://www.debonogroup.com/six_thinking_hats.php

Towers Watson, "2014 Global Workforce Study," http://www.towerswatson.com/en-US/Insights/IC-Types/Survey-Research-Results/2014/08/the-2014-global-workforce-study

Project Management Institute, "Organizational Agility, 2012"http://www.pmi.org/~/media/PDF/Research/Organizational-Agility-In-Depth-Report.ashx

APPENDIX B:

Acknowledgments

Our book has been a labor of love that has taken a number of years to complete due mostly to the passion we have for working with our clients. We are very fortunate to have many long-term relationships with clients across many industries and geographies. Our thanks go out to all of them as they have been important contributors to the insights, nuances, and practical applications of our Agile Model and inspired much of the content in this book.

In addition, we appreciate the contributions and participation of our affiliated colleagues across the Unites States and beyond. Each of these colleagues brings unique richness and talents to the conversation and have helped clients gain traction in creating agility advantage. In particular, Ben Baran has been an invaluable thought partner as he has led our research-based efforts to validate existing tools and in developing a new series of assessments related to employee engagement and the expansive field of agility personality profile. We also would like to recognize Mike Richardson, San Diego based friend and colleague, who we have worked closely with during the past year and even more closely as we merge our businesses.

Thanks also go to a number of friends, clients, and colleagues who have helped with our practice development, thought leadership, and manuscript development in various ways including Bo Kenan, Justo Nunez, Kathy Hanna, Steve Sakats, David and Donna Van Eekeren, Mark Nelson, Gary McKinney, Mary Eckenrod, Joel Katz, Bob Prescott, Brian Anderson, Mark Haas, Stephen Patrick, Martin Wilcox, Sherre De Mao, Walt Pilcher, Sean O'Shea as well as Henry and Devin DeVries from our publishing house.

Our families have been steady supporters and important sources of encouragement including Chandler and Amanda Horney as well as Louise, Kevin, and Ryan O'Shea. Tom's daughter, Meaghan O'Shea Clayton, manages our newsletter and social media communications while keeping Tom centered. There is no question that our biggest supporter, master administrator, and most valued business partner is Rhonda Horney, Nick's better half. Rhonda has been an integral part of Agility Consulting since the firm began in 2001. She is the epitome of agility—always focused, fast, and flexible. Our success would not be possible without Rhonda's dedication, patience, and care.

APPENDIX C:

About the Authors

Nick Horney, PhD

Nick Horney founded Agility Consulting and Training in 2001 and has been recognized for innovations in the fields of leadership and change management. He has consulted with global leaders to help transform their vision to action by anticipating change and building more adaptive capabilities. Dr. Horney has been recognized as an expert in strategic agility by journals such as *People & Strategy* and *CIO Magazine*, books such as *Human Resource Transformation* (2008) and organizations such as the American Management Association, Canadian Management Centre, IBN International, Human Resource People and Strategy, and AMA Japan.

Dr. Horney co-authored a book in 2000 entitled *Project Change Management*, published by McGraw-Hill. His first-hand knowledge of agility and change management was developed during his twenty-three years as a Navy Special Operations officer leading diving and explosive ordnance disposal teams where change was a daily event.

Tom O'Shea, MS, CMC

A proven expert in organizational agility, Tom O'Shea has over two decades real-world experience working in consumer products, retailing, and the apparel trade with industry leading companies. His diverse background includes senior executive roles in human resources, strategic planning, and general management. He has been VP/GM for a large consumer-products division developing and marketing products across all classes of retail trade, which helped him develop keen insights into the keys to success in real-time, consumer-driven enterprises.

He has provided skillful direction and team-based solutions for complex issues and scenarios in the U.S. and abroad. He has also been a trusted advisor to numerous business leaders and client organizations for over fifteen years, providing coaching or consulting to a very diverse set of organizations across many industries and geographies.

APPENDIX D:

Creating Your Agility Profile™

Ben Baran, PhD, Agility Analytics Practice Leader

Thriving in a volatile, uncertain, complex and ambiguous (VUCA) world requires a sharp focus on the right priorities. And the way to achieve that clarity is through keen measurement and analytics. Agility Analytics is one of the four practice areas in Agility Consulting & Training (ACT) and the research and assessments in our analytics toolbox weave across each of our other practice areas: Leadership Agility, Team Agility and Organizational Agility.

Agility Analytics is a core strength of what we do and provides us a rigorous, fact-based foundation for each of our practice areas:

- Produces original research studies and reports on agility and supporting topics

- Synthesizes cutting-edge research and thought regarding agility from around the globe

- Develops new user-friendly ways for people and organizations to measure agility while continually refining our current instruments

Through our Agility Analytics, we help people and organizations become more focused, fast and flexible by measuring their current state, determining improvement priorities, designing change transformations and measuring progress.

Our Agility Assessment Portfolio™ includes:

- Leadership Agility Profile™ 360 Assessment

- Agility Personality Profile™

- Team Agility Profile™, and the

- Organizational Agility Profile™

Above all, Agility Analytics is about providing the solutions necessary to cut through the fog of ambiguity that's become common in our VUCA world.

SPECIAL GIFT WITH PURCHASE OF THE BOOK … go to www.focusedfastandflexible.com and enter promotion code MYAGILITY go get your free Leadership Agility Profile Self-Assessment Results.

We also provide you an abbreviated worksheet here you can use for yourself, your team or organizational assessment.

Below is a framework you can use to conduct a self-assessment for leadership, team or organizational agility. *THE AGILE MODEL*® drivers and capabilities provide a diagnostic schematic for examining proficiency or development needs around the critical constructs that build focused, fast and flexible leaders, teams and organizations. You can apply this framework to your assessment of individual leaders (including yourself), operating or project teams as well as the overall enterprise by setting the context for those involved in the sharing feedback.

MY SELF & TEAM AGILITY PROFILE

			SELF	TEAM
Anticipating Change	1.	**Visioning:** Creating a clear mental picture of what the future could be and engineering that vision into everyday activities for myself and my team.		
	2.	**Sensing:** Recognizing the forces that can disrupt or impede success and creating early warning indicators to signal impending change.		
	3.	**Monitoring:** Identifying, collecting, organizing, and documenting information to help track patterns and trends associated with factors that impact our success.		
Generating Confidence	4.	**Connecting:** Influencing self and others to be excited, enthused, and committed to advancing the organization's objectives and awareness for how all stakeholders contribute to success.		
	5.	**Aligning:** Ensuring the right balance of resources, energy and priorities are present to achieve successful, values based solutions and results ... even in dynamic situations.		
	6.	**Engaging:** Building positive emotional connection by encouraging and getting greater discretionary team effort and involvement for the success of the team and organization.		

			SELF	TEAM
Initiating Action	7.	**Bias for Action:** Operating with proactive sense of urgency driven by a real desire to makes things better for customers and organization.		
	8.	**Decision-Making:** Using a systematic and rapid approach for making decisions and effectively solving problems that operates fluidly and naturally at all levels within the organization.		
	9.	**Collaboration:** Actively and positively interacting with others within and outside the department to seek and give information so the organization can regularly create better ideas and solutions.		
Liberating Thinking	10.	**Bias for Innovation:** Seeking and encouraging fresh innovative thinking for solving problems and improving products and services for the benefit of customers and the organization.		
	11.	**Customer Focus:** Developing solutions in a manner that demonstrates an understanding of internal and external customers' needs and desire for timely, cost-effective and value-added services.		
	12.	**Idea Diversity:** Seeking a variety of perspectives in an open-minded manner from traditional and nontraditional sources; seeks alternative, new or nontraditional approaches from all levels and stakeholders.		
Evaluating Results	13.	**Creating Expectations:** Clearly defining customer driven expected outcomes for self and all team members to create a good understanding to guide performance and achieve desired results.		
	14.	**Real-Time Feedback:** Regularly giving and receiving important communication or feedback with team members and customers in a positive, productive and timely manner.		
	15.	**Fact-Based Measures:** Using good data and information in a clear, rational and thorough process to understand issues, evaluating options, forming accurate conclusions and making decisions.		

AGILITY PROFILE™ TOTAL SCORE	SELF	TEAM
1 = need much improvement 2 = need improvement 3 = competent 4 = strength area 5 = major strength area		
How Can You Improve Your Agility?		

CONTINUE	START	STOP

PLOT YOUR AGILITY PROFILE™ SELF-ASSESSMENT

Place your self rating on the axis of each Agililty capability — outer ring = 5

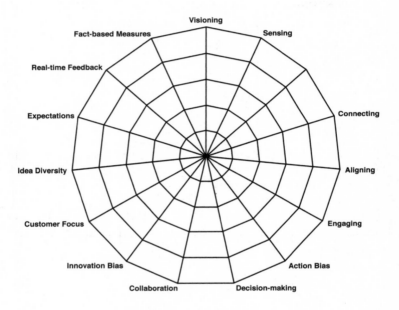

Copyright Agility Consulting & Training, LLC

Once you have completed your Self and Team Agility assessments, you can transfer your ratings on the Agility Profile spydergram. Place a dot on the axis of each of the fifteen agility capabilities at the intersection of vertical and horizontal axis to reflect our rating with rating of five would be on the outer ring and one would be on the inner ring. Then you should draw a line between the dots to create your Agility Profile for Self and Team.

INDEX